BUMPER STICKER Wisdom

America's Pulpit Above the Tailpipe

Carol W. Gardner

BEYOND
WORDS
Publishing
I N C

Beyond Words Publishing, Inc. (whose owners' bumper stickers read "When the people lead, the leaders will follow" and "Create peace")
4443 NE Airport Road
Hillsboro, Oregon 97124-6074
503-693-8700
1-800-284-9673

Editor: Michelle Roehm (whose bumper sticker reads "Honk once if you're Jesus—honk twice if you're Elvis")
Design and layout: Principia Graphica (They're far too cool for bumper stickers.)
Proofreading: Hemidemisemiquaver (Marvin Moore of HDSQ rides a bicycle with a tiny sticker that says "Car-free zones now!")

Manufactured in China
Distributed to the book trade by Publishers Group West (As book distributors go, PGW is indisputably the best. We don't know what their stickers say, but here's one we wrote for them: "It's hard to be humble when you work for PGW.")

Library of Congress Cataloging-in-Publication Data
Gardner, Carol W.
    Bumper sticker wisdom : America's pulpit above the tailpipe /
Carol W. Gardner.
        p.   cm.
    Interviews, with photographs.
    ISBN 1-885223-17-X (trade paper)
    1. Aphorisms and apothegms.   2. Bumper stickers.   3. American wit
and humor.   I. Title.
    PN6271.G37   1995
    818'.520208—dc20   95-15686
                                    CIP

The Library of Congress is far too big to list every bumper sticker, but we have one for them: "I ♥ the Dewey decimal system."

Best reason to have a bumper sticker on your vehicle: You get to meet Carol Gardner and be in a cool book that lets you go on and on about gun control and whirled peas.

Best reason *not* to have a bumper sticker on your vehicle: You might accidentally meet Carol Gardner in a parking lot and waste your fifteen minutes of fame in a book that lets you go on and on about gun control and whirled peas.

The corporate mission of Beyond Words Publishing, Inc.: *Inspire to Integrity*

Dedicated
to
James and Jay

ACKNOWLEDGMENTS

First and foremost I would like to thank the people who are featured in *Bumper Sticker Wisdom*. Their good humor and generosity taught me a lot about tolerance. Obviously I couldn't agree with all of them on the issues they put forth on their bumper stickers, but I discovered that I liked, enjoyed, and laughed with even those with whom I disagreed. It is my hope that this effect transfers to the readers of this book.

Many people who aren't mentioned in this book deserve a thank you, from Chris Linenbroker, who works in the camera department at K-Mart in Liberal, Kansas, and who repaired my camera after a dust storm had ground the shutter to a halt, to the people I met around the country who so generously invited me into their homes for pan-fried chicken lunches or to join them for burgers at local drive-ins.

In addition, I would like to thank my friends. First, Kathy Van Raden, who not only traveled with me to Beaver, Oklahoma, for the World Champion Cow Chip Throw but who entered the contest and came in fourth! Also thanks to Bob and Nani Warren, whose great sense of humor has always been an inspiration. Thanks also go to all my "bumper sticker stalkers," including Vernon and Marion Alden in Boston, Chic Slepian in New York, and Elliot Richardson in Washington, D.C.

I am grateful, also, to Kirk Sidley, Scott Johnson, and Kelly Gillingham at Picture Perfect for helping me develop the photographic souvenirs of my travels.

Most of all, thanks go to my husband, James, who traveled with me from New England to New Mexico and who has always been supportive of my antics, no matter how bizarre, and to our 16-year-old son, Jay, who sacrificed much of his free time to help me record my bumper sticker adventures on the computer and who only rolled his eyes a few times as I sprinted across parking lots chasing bumper stickers.

I am also deeply indebted to Richard Cohn, Cindy Black, Michelle Roehm (my editor and the brave soul who accompanied me to Graceland, Opryland, and Bucksnort, Tennessee) and to all my other wonderful friends at Beyond Words Publishing, Inc., and Principia Graphica. I especially appreciated the balance between their professionalism and fun.

An unusual thank you I'd like to include goes to Dr. John Dennis, the neurosurgeon who saved my life many years ago by removing a blood clot from my brain. There are those who question whether or not he saved my sanity. The vote is still out on that one.

Finally, my heartfelt thanks to my parents, Russell and Ardyce Lentz, for the love and support they have always given me, even when I've shocked them (see Buck and Hooter on page 22).

TABLE OF CONTENTS

This is a book about bumper stickers and the people behind them. It is a portrait of America: a nation of people in automobiles—that ultimate national icon—on the move with stickers expressing a view, sharing a frustration, or offering some perceived insight, solution, or wisdom. Mobility, technology, personality, and free expression, all in one. What could be more American?

Bumper stickers. You see them virtually every day, offering one or another pronouncement. They are at the same time so outspoken and yet discreet, so public and yet personal, and always so anonymous. Each bumper sticker leads to countless questions: What does it mean? To whom is it addressed? Why did someone put it on their car?

The very inquiry points to the deeper mystery and magic of bumper stickers. It is not merely the message but the messenger that is so fascinating. Who *are* these people who have such a desire to share their opinions with you? How does their personality fit their pronouncement? What are their lives like? What is the message they seek to convey? What are their likes and dislikes? Above all, what compels them to hold forth from the bumper of their car?

They sit there behind their wheel, and in front of you, driving down the streets, roads, and freeways of America. They don't know you or your views, and in reality that's not the issue—for bumper stickers are an exercise of expression, not listening. In all probability they are driving along thinking of something other than that bold pronouncement they affixed to their bumper many months or years before. Often they had not even been planning to make a statement until they saw the particular saying of their choice, at which point it was love at first sight, as though just that sentiment had been awaiting a form of release and expression. Almost without exception, however, the message is important to them and touches on something they are anxious to speak about.

The bumper sticker may be an expression of personal philosophy, political anger and outrage, religious conviction, parental pride, sexual preference, or social comment. It may represent a simple statement of personal humor, ethnic identity, or class resentment. It may offer views of the opposite sex and marriage or of American culture and social institutions. What did that nice little lady in Idaho mean when she affixed to her car a bumper sticker that stated "Divorce . . . the screwing you get for the screwing you got"? If you ask her, as I did, the chances are she will tell you—a lot.

Bumper stickers do not emerge in a vacuum but within the era and political culture of which they are a part. They change with time and region and public discussion. Differing bumper stickers offer conflicting perspectives, and they may eventually engender a bumper sticker response. To a "Save the whales" sticker comes the response, "Save the humans," which in turn brings forth even a third snappy comeback, "To hell with whales—save the cowboy!" Thus, there is a kind of a dialogue of the drivers that goes on out there, a "town hall" of the American roadways.

Bumper stickers also offer an easy platform for everyday citizens to express frustration and criticism, not infrequently at the expense of politicians, including the president. This book was researched and written primarily during the Clinton administration, resulting in a good number of comments, often unflattering, being directed at the president and, for the first time, the first lady. This, too, reflects the mood of the nation—and quite possibly some deep cultural tensions surrounding changing roles of women. It also says a lot about the American character and treatment of presidents. A few years ago one would have found similar critical bumper stickers for presidents Nixon, Reagan, and Bush. And future presidents, both Republican and Democrat, will surely feel the heat of bumper sticker criticism, too. I've tried to be fair and balanced in my representation of political bumper stickers, and at the same time honest in reflecting trends in one direction or another.

Occasionally, presidents themselves are even drawn to this national passion for bumper sticker simplification and sound bites. Before a trip to Russia, for example, President Clinton declared, "The bumper sticker for this trip will be 'More reform, more aid'"—American foreign policy, announced as a bumper sticker! Similarly, during the last election and just before he lost the White House, President Bush railed against bias in the media and offered his own solution: "You know my favorite bumper sticker, 'Annoy the media, re-elect Bush.'" So presidents get their bumper sticker say, too.

The reaction to bumper sticker pronouncements is also interesting. There are very few bumper stickers out there that don't elicit some reaction from passersby—that is one of the main reasons for having one. Every bumper sticker owner has stories of people driving by laughing, giving them a thumbs-up, shaking their fist, or flipping them off. But I have been surprised to learn about the numerous occasions that bumper stickers have led to recrimination, legal action, and even violence. In Oregon a construction worker says he lost his job on a university site because of his anti-gay bumper stickers. In Louisiana and Georgia the state legislatures enacted anti-obscenity and speech codes applicable to bumper stickers, leading one enterprising individual to paraphrase the "Shit happens" bumper sticker with "Doo-doo occurs." And in Kentucky the driver of a pickup truck with a rebel flag was killed in a racially motivated attack. Even in the seemingly innocuous world of bumper stickers, freedom of speech can be a dangerous game.

This book has been researched and written in a spirit of genuine curiosity and of real and growing appreciation for the owners and declarants of "bumper sticker wisdom." For more than a year I have traveled the roadways of this country, from Maine to Arizona, from Oregon to Florida. My research and travel carried me from the White House to the National Cow Chip Throw in Beaver, Oklahoma, and the Mosquito Festival in Paisley, Oregon. I was able to visit such meccas as Graceland, Opryland, and Bucksnort, Tennessee. On Cape Cod I met a sea captain who had attached an "I brake for whales" sticker to his boat and a commercial oyster fisherman whose bumper sticker said "Eat'm raw!"—as indeed he had. In Indian, Alaska, a local resident's bumper sticker suggested we "Eat moose—40,000 brown bears can't be wrong!" while in Harvard Square an academic advised us to "Subvert the dominant paradigm." In Santa Fe a young man offered "Fukengrüven," while in Chicago a driver declared "Snow happens!" I met a good-humored bachelor from Utah who joked about local customs with "Single Mormon seeks several spouses," while in Hollywood, an aspiring actor also joked about local customs with "Will act for food." Everywhere there are unique bumper sticker perspectives and people shaped by their surroundings.

I have engaged in the art of bumper sticker stalking. In the process I have waved down and pulled over farmers and retirees, Indians and cowboys, hippies and yuppies, migrant workers and minorities, scientists and authors, stockbrokers and professionals, parents and families on vacation, laborers and housewives shopping. These are not the nightly news anchors or figures of national influence; they are the everyday citizens and real people who make up America. I have found that most bumper sticker owners are generous with their time and sentiments, and frequently they're flattered by an interest in their perspective. Talkative nation and people that we are, bumper sticker owners are often anxious to share their views.

My strongest impression has been of the underlying diversity and vitality of bumper sticker pronouncements. There is virtually no end to the views expressed. And the people behind the expressions proved to be endlessly interesting and ever so anxious to hold forth on their lives and views. Often they would think long and hard on an answer expressed, and sometimes they would call me later with an amendment or an additional reflection. I've tried to honor that implicit act of trust by presenting the respective views fairly and honestly.

The best part about writing *Bumper Sticker Wisdom* is that I came to learn more about myself. I realized that I had been moving in a circle of friends that seemed like-minded and homogenous. I reaffirmed that America is indeed peopled by a remarkably diverse array of individuals, often with conflicting and strongly held views. Finally—and most importantly—I discovered that people may hold diametrically opposing views and still be good people. I found I really liked individuals with whom I strongly disagreed on one or another issue. So my conclusion is this: It's great to speak out. It's OK to disagree. It's healthy to respect and leave room for other perspectives, and for humanity and humor. I think tolerance is the ultimate "bumper sticker wisdom."

I hope you enjoy this book. I've had a wonderful time writing it and learning about the people behind the bumper stickers. There is sure to be a bumper sticker in here that goes contrary to everything you believe in—and another that fits you to a T. For the record, my personal favorite is "Enjoy life—this is not a rehearsal!" but your favorite is sure to be different. You certainly don't have to agree with all the views offered here to appreciate the right to "freedom of expression" that is being exercised—it would probably be unhealthy if not impossible to agree with them all. In fact, I would dedicate this book to the important constitutional rights these expressions so modestly but popularly reflect and to the humor, angst, and perspectives of the bumper sticker owners I have met throughout this land. I am deeply appreciative for their generosity and verbosity!

But the reader should stand forewarned: Bumper stickers can become addictive! I am confident that once you have been through *Bumper Sticker Wisdom*, you will become a more active observer and participant in this strange and wondrous dialogue of American drivers. Beyond that, I will let the bumper stickers and their owners speak for themselves.

Carol W. Gardner

I OWE, I OWE
SO OFF TO WORK I GO

♥ MY BOSS ♥ MY JOB
I'M SELF EMPLOYED

THE DAILY
COMMUTE
(WORK)

I'M NOT A BUM,
MY WIFE WORKS!

Kick a Lawyer To

PHRESH STICKERS (503) 285-6539

MICHELE DAVIS

AGE: 25
EDUCATION: Bend High School
OCCUPATION: Employee at McDonald's
FAVORITE PASTIMES: Skiing, horseback riding, bike riding, watching television, and reading
FAVORITE BOOK: *The Tommyknockers* by Stephen King
FAVORITE MOVIE: *When Harry Met Sally*
PET PEEVE: "Dirty stove tops—I hate it!"

BUMPER STICKER *Wisdom* "I had a boss at McDonald's who was just a total jerk. I thought this bumper sticker was perfect. He would just die if he saw this on the back of my car. He was really arrogant, demanding, and self-centered—the most egotistical man I've ever met, and he made me feel like I was nothing."

HAPPINESS IS SEEING YOUR BOSS' PICTURE ON THE BACK OF A MILK CARTON!!

J&P Products
San Diego, Ca

AGE: 61
OCCUPATION: Contractor
FAVORITE PASTIMES: Work and going to the horse races
FAVORITE BOOK: The Bible
FAVORITE MOVIE: *The Hanging Tree*
PET PEEVE: My wife

FRANK ORTEGA

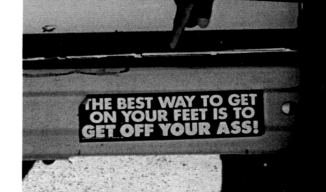

THE BEST WAY TO GET ON YOUR FEET IS TO GET OFF YOUR ASS!

© PROFIT PLUS NOVELTY CO. PONTIAC, MI.

BUMPER STICKER *Wisdom* "I'm trying to tell people to get to work! Don't sit around and wait for things to come to you. You have to work like I do. And get ahead like I did. I'm bragging now!"

THE BEST WAY TO GET ON YOUR FEET IS TO GET OFF YOUR ASS!

11

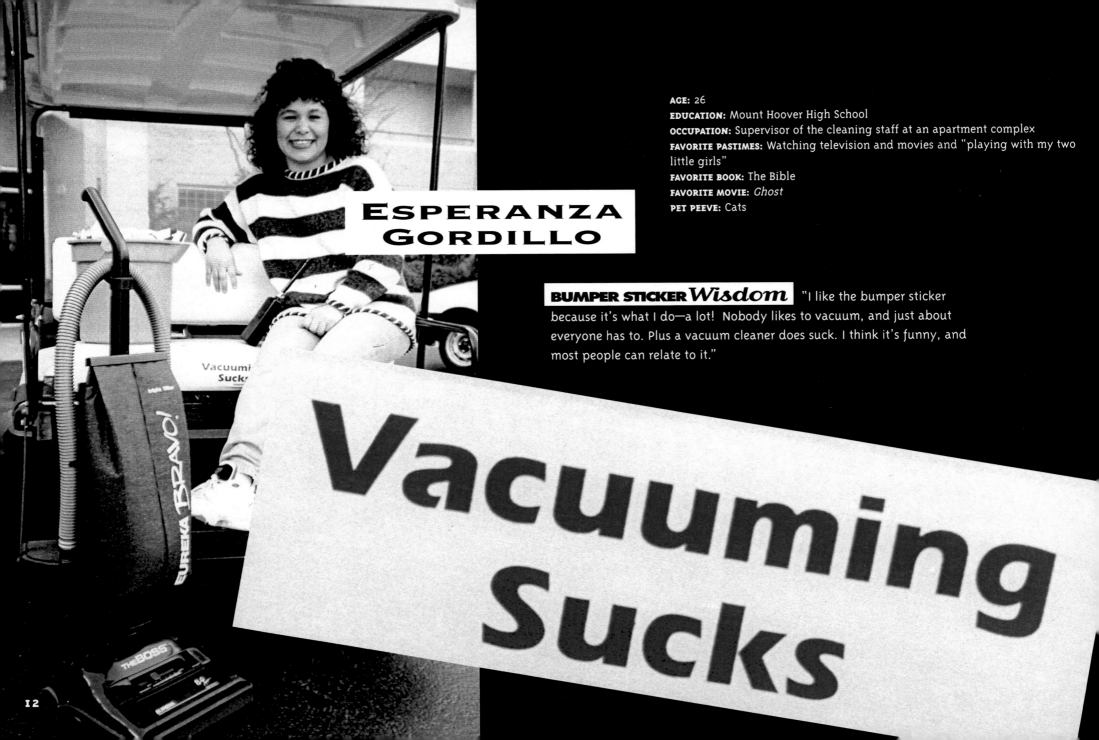

ESPERANZA GORDILLO

AGE: 26

EDUCATION: Mount Hoover High School

OCCUPATION: Supervisor of the cleaning staff at an apartment complex

FAVORITE PASTIMES: Watching television and movies and "playing with my two little girls"

FAVORITE BOOK: The Bible

FAVORITE MOVIE: *Ghost*

PET PEEVE: Cats

BUMPER STICKER *Wisdom* — "I like the bumper sticker because it's what I do—a lot! Nobody likes to vacuum, and just about everyone has to. Plus a vacuum cleaner does suck. I think it's funny, and most people can relate to it."

Vacuuming Sucks

JAMES A. WATSON

AGE: 59
EDUCATION: Shreveport Vocational Tech School
OCCUPATION: Chief sales clerk at a surplus store
FAVORITE PASTIMES: Wood carving, working in the yard, and sword collecting
FAVORITE BOOK: *Shogun* by James Clavell
FAVORITE MOVIE: *Star Trek*
PET PEEVE: Inconsistency in people

I FIGHT POVERTY, — I WORK —

BUMPER STICKER *Wisdom* "After more than 10 years at Tektronix, I got laid off in April of 1988. I couldn't get any job back in the field I was in at Tektronix, so I said the hell with it, I'm going to start out at the bottom again. I got a job at K-Mart at $4.25 an hour. These guys offered me a job here at Aloha Surplus with better pay, and I've been here a little over three years now.

"I think people who live off welfare are slugs. You look at videos showing Baloney Joe's [a shelter for the homeless in Portland, Oregon] at Thanksgiving, and 99 percent of them are fat. OK, if I saw them down there all gaunt and hungry-looking, I'd be all for it. Those are people who just don't want to work. There are jobs every-where, you know. If you're not picky, you find you can do all kinds of things."

I FIGHT POVERTY, — I WORK —

Author's Note: Jim is a man full of determination despite some hard times in the job market. He is proud that he has pulled himself up by his own bootstraps time and time again, and he is strongly critical of others who have not done the same. He is looking forward to retirement in a couple of years and to having more time to spend wood carving.

DEFUNDING EDUCATION IS
DEFEATING THE FUTURE

DONNELLY COLT CUSTOMPRINTING, BOX 188 HAMPTON, CT 06247 203-455-9621

IF YOU CAN READ THIS
THANK A MUSIC TEACHER

SLOW, CHILDREN
AHEAD
(FAMILY AND EDUCATION)

IF IT'S NOT ONE THING
IT'S YOUR MOTHER

it will be a great day when our
schools get all the money they
need and the air force has to
hold a bake sale to buy a bomber

MOTHER IN-LAW IN TRUNK

CAMERON KERR

AGE: 45
EDUCATION: Briar Cliff College
OCCUPATION: Mother
FAVORITE PASTIMES: The outdoors and her children
FAVORITE MOVIE: *Out of Africa*
PET PEEVE: Teachers who like to go by their first names

BUMPER STICKER *Wisdom* "I think everybody should know that education is worth every penny you put into it. I love watching people behind me, especially when there is like a teenager or an adolescent in the car with their parents."

Author's Note: Cameron is the mother of four children and was just leaving a supermarket on the way to pick up the two youngest girls from school. Her children attend a private school, and she has decided the added expense is worth it.

If You Think Education Is Expensive, Try Ignorance

AGE: 51

EDUCATION: Portland State University (art education)

OCCUPATION: Ethnic-student advisor at Portland State University, working primarily with Native American students

FAVORITE PASTIMES: Making things with her hands, crafts, painting, watercolor, sewing, and reading

FAVORITE BOOK: *Neuromancer* by William Gibson

FAVORITE MOVIE: *Doctor Zhivago* and *Crooklyn*

PET PEEVE: When stores put price tags on items that are impossible to remove, e.g., the sticky tags on glass items

I'M THE PROUD PARENT OF A GRANT HIGH SCHOOL HONOR STUDENT

BUMPER STICKER *Wisdom* "This bumper sticker is from last year. My son, Zack, was a freshman, and I thought that he did really well. I felt very good that he came in as a freshman and was able to accomplish what he did. I thought it was very commendable on his part. I was really proud as a parent.

"I probably embarass Zack by putting it on our car, but that's all right. I think it's great when a kid does well, and I want to reinforce that."

BEV SOKOL

AGE: 40
EDUCATION: Portland State University (art)
OCCUPATION: Owner of Book Props (sales of props to teachers and librarians)
FAVORITE PASTIMES: Making jewelry and reading
FAVORITE BOOK: *Turn: The Journal of an Artist* by Anne Truitt
FAVORITE MOVIE: *A Thousand Clowns*
PET PEEVE: "When my husband mixes the colored clothes with the white clothes in the laundry"

BUMPER STICKER *Wisdom* "The bumper sticker was given to me by my friend Susan. She knew I'd love it. Actually, the best part is seeing my child, Max, next to the bumper sticker, because he's in seventh grade and he's about three and a half feet tall. The bumper sticker is kind of a reaction to all those cars with bumper stickers that say 'My child is an honor student at such and such a school.' I've had a hundred people stop me on the street asking, 'Where did you get that?'"

MY KID
BEAT UP YOUR HONOR STUDENT

AGE: 21
EDUCATION: Portland Community College (graphic design)
OCCUPATION: Graphic designer
FAVORITE PASTIMES: Listening to and absorbing music
FAVORITE BOOK: *Catcher in the Rye* by J. D. Salinger
FAVORITE MOVIE: *Yellow Submarine*
PET PEEVE: Liars

MATT ERCEG

BUMPER STICKER *Wisdom*

"I think it's great if someone's kid is an honor-roll student, but I don't think they need to show the world.

MY SON KNOCKED UP YOUR HONOR ROLL STUDENT

I think it's kind of like bragging. Not my taste. My bumper stickers are a reaction to those. I was going to try to sell them on the street, but people either walked by and gave me little snears or they walked by and laughed. No one really bought them.

"I was a 'C' student, and my parents didn't have a bumper sticker that said 'My kid is a C student.'"

MY KID SOLD DRUGS TO YOUR HONOR ROLL STUDENT

MY SON KNOCKED UP YOUR HONOR ROLL STUDENT

AGE: 58
EDUCATION: San Jacinto High School
OCCUPATION: Senior funder for mortgages at a bank
FAVORITE PASTIMES: Shopping, dancing, music, theater, and "looking for Mr. Right"
FAVORITE BOOK: Books by Leo Buscaglia
FAVORITE MOVIE: *Pretty Woman*
PET PEEVE: People who don't follow through with what they say

JANE KRICHEVSKY

BUMPER STICKER *Wisdom* "The car was not mine originally. It belonged to friends of mine. When I bought it, it came with the bumper sticker. We tried to get it off because they wanted it for their two schnauzers. It wouldn't come off, so that's how I got it.

"I only have one dog now, but I feel that she is an honor student. She sits, she stays, she seems to mind except when it comes to chewing. I just love her, and she has filled a void in my life."

My Dogs Are Honor Students

JENNI O'LEARY

AGE: 20
EDUCATION: David Douglas High School
OCCUPATION: Receptionist
FAVORITE PASTIMES: "Playing with my computer"
FAVORITE BOOK: *Nightmares & Dreamscapes* by Stephen King
FAVORITE MOVIE: *Interview with a Vampire*
PET PEEVE: Weak women

BUMPER STICKER *Wisdom* "I just started calling my dad an 'old fart' one day, so he bought me the bumper sticker.

"An old fart is a middle-aged, middle-class, old person. It's positive, affectionate. You know, a married man with a couple of kids, in his fifties, who lounges around the house. He loves his family and tries to take care of them. He has a good sense of humor.

"Old farts like to tinker with things. My dad has a whole garage full of tinker toys."

20

TERRI MAHAFFEY

AGE: 33
EDUCATION: Metro Beauty School
OCCUPATION: Homemaker
FAVORITE PASTIMES: Being outdoors and golfing
FAVORITE BOOK: *Once in a Lifetime* by Danielle Steele
FAVORITE MOVIE: *The Bodyguard*
PET PEEVE: Dirty underwear on the floor

BUMPER STICKER *Wisdom* "I always tell my kids, 'I'm the mom, that's why,' and you get that from your mother. I put it on the truck, and people will think, 'Man, I've heard that so many times.' It's a never-ending quote. As long as there are mothers, it will always be there."

I'm The Mommy That's Why

Author's Note: I met Terri in Amarillo, Texas. Her bumper sticker really captured her personality—sunny, full of good humor, and very much a mommy.

I'm The Mommy That's Why

RICK & SAMI KRUMPECK

AGE: 37 (Rick) / 35 (Sami)
EDUCATION: William S. Hart High School / West Valley High School
OCCUPATION: Utility dispatcher / housewife
FAVORITE PASTIMES: Horseback riding, barrel racing, travel, and camping
FAVORITE BOOK: *Sahara* by Clive Cussler / mysteries by J. A. Jance
FAVORITE MOVIE: *The Fugitive* / *It's a Wonderful Life*
PET PEEVE: Phony people / Dishonesty and crimes against animals

BUMPER STICKER *Wisdom* "'Nudist families have more fun' is the way our lifestyle is. We take off, go on vacation, and off come the clothes. Who cares? That's the way we were born, that's the way we feel.

"Just last year we went to Snoqualmie Nudist Park for the Bare Buns Fun Run. There were 500 people running a 5K race through the mountains.

NUDIST FAMILIES HAVE MORE FUN

FRATERNITY SNOQUALMIE...(206) 392-NUDE

It was a wonderful day.

"For nudists there are no barriers. Shape and age don't matter. If someone walks up to you dressed a particular way, immediately you make a judgment. With nudists, you meet someone and status doesn't matter.

"Our favorite game at home is strip horseshoes in the back yard. Two years ago a neighbor called the police because [Rick] was riding the lawn mower naked. Our neighbors live a half mile away and so the officer said the neighbors must have binoculars.

"[Rick's] nickname is 'Buck' for buck naked, and my nickname is 'Hoot' for hooters. Our friends just call us Buck and Hoot."

I LOVE CATS
They Taste Just Like Chicken

Save the Spotted Cow

ANIMAL XING
(ANIMALS)

EAT MOOSE
40,000 BROWN BEARS CAN'T BE WRONG!

BROWN BEAR SALOON
INDIAN, ALASKA
MILE 103 SEWARD HWY
653-7000

Humans aren't the only species
on earth - We just act like it

© 1993, NORTHERN SUN MERCHANDISING

**TO HELL WITH
THE DOG
BEWARE OF
THE OWNER!!!**

© 85 J&P Products

DAVID PAINE

AGE: 36
EDUCATION: Nauset Regional High School
OCCUPATION: Commercial fisherman
FAVORITE PASTIMES: Work, trail-bike riding, and motorcycles
FAVORITE BOOK: *Cape Cod Times* (newspaper)
FAVORITE MOVIE: *Butch Cassidy and the Sundance Kid*
PET PEEVE: People who don't know where they are going and people in a hurry

BUMPER STICKER *Wisdom* "I put the bumper sticker on my boat in 1987. We were fishing off Nantucket. There was a good crop of scallops out there, and I'd never seen so many whales in my life. They were coming up beside us just everywhere. We went into Nantucket to get some supplies, and I was walking by this shop when I saw this sticker, 'I brake for whales.' I thought, 'This is perfect.' It's been on my boat ever since."

I BRAKE for WHALES

SHELDON HENTSCHKE

AGE: 66
EDUCATION: University of Southern California
OCCUPATION: Real-estate agent and retired educator
FAVORITE PASTIMES: Living in the mountains
FAVORITE BOOK: Magazines
FAVORITE MOVIE: *Quo Vadis?*
PET PEEVE: Myself for taking on other people's peeving

BUMPER STICKER *Wisdom* "I have a great-looking ridgeback dog named Zambezi, and I entered him in a dog show, and, you know, they disqualified him because his testicles hadn't dropped. So I bought him this bumper sticker."

UNLESS YOU ARE THE LEAD DOG—THE VIEW IS ALWAYS THE SAME

Author's Note: *I thought Sheldon was going to tell me how he had left the masses behind in L.A. and had fled to the mountains of Idaho with his rugged individualism. Instead, he told me about his dog.*

Author's Note: I interviewed Megan at a filbert farm with her two potbellied pig friends, Moe and Joe. If you ask me, Megan is a lot better-looking than Moe and Joe.

AGE: 25
EDUCATION: Lewis and Clark College (communications)
OCCUPATION: Student, working part-time, wants to be arts administrator for aquariums
FAVORITE PASTIMES: Outdoors, hiking, bike riding, fishing, garage sales, mixed-media art
FAVORITE BOOK: *To Kill a Mockingbird* by Harper Lee
FAVORITE MOVIE: *La Femme Nikita*
PET PEEVE: Indecisiveness

BUMPER STICKER *Wisdom*   "I've been interested in pigs since the second grade. I was visiting my brother, who was back in school in Boston, when I saw this bumper sticker in a store and said, 'Yes!' I wanted to see if it would get a reaction from people, and it has. Some people who are related to policemen have asked me about the bumper sticker, if I like the animal, or if I like the people connected with that term. I've gotten some pretty fun reactions. People usually claim pigs are ugly, but I go, 'No, they're not!'"

Honk if you love pigs

TONY HILL

AGE: 30
EDUCATION: Nauset High School
OCCUPATION: Fishing
FAVORITE PASTIMES: "Whatever you can imagine"
FAVORITE MOVIE: *Rocky* movies
PET PEEVE: "I'm easygoing that way—I guess I don't have any pet peeves."

EAT'M RAW!
ROSE OYSTERS, WELLFLEET, MA
(508) 349-7859

BUMPER STICKER *Wisdom* "I got the bumper sticker from a guy I used to fish with. He and I do a lot of oysters, and I've fished with him for a long time. He had a few bumper stickers made up, and I stuck it on my truck when I bought it. I loved it. I thought it was awesome. I fish for oysters, clams, and scallops, and you better believe I eat'm raw. That's the only way to eat'm."

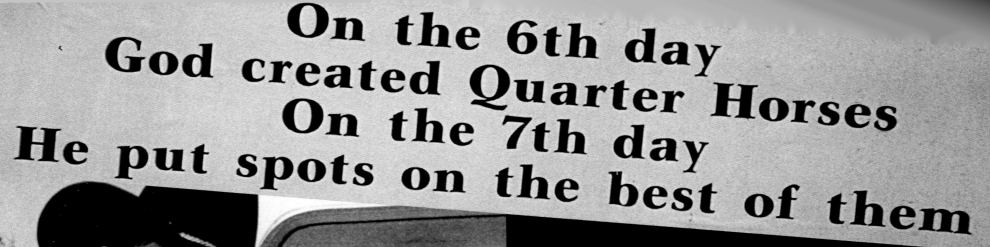

On the 6th day God created Quarter Horses On the 7th day He put spots on the best of them

AGE: 52
EDUCATION: University of Oregon (business)
OCCUPATION: Real-estate developer
FAVORITE PASTIMES: Fishing, golf, horses, and fly tying
FAVORITE BOOK: *Green Hills of Africa* by Ernest Hemingway
FAVORITE MOVIE: *A River Runs Through It*
PET PEEVE: "Government intervention into our lives and private citizens trying to dictate how we live"

BUMPER STICKER *Wisdom* "The bumper sticker, 'On the 6th day God created quarter horses—on the 7th day he put spots on the best of them,' is a play on a biblical phrase, and it points out what I think is the most beautiful domesticated animal—the paint horse.

"Raising and breeding paint horses has been a recent avocation which was instigated by my 13-year-old daughter. It has contributed greatly to our happiness."

MICK HUMPHREYS

JEFFREY D. FOWLER

cker *Wisdom* "The greatest significance of my
r me is that my dog, Dottie, is a guide dog. She is a very spe-
he is the only Akita to have gone to Guide Dog School in the
d she was chosen Guide Dog of the Year last year. She was on
w her to New York, and she has been written up extensively.
e important thing about Dottie is that, in contrast to the people
Dottie is constantly devoted, constantly dependable, con-
ntly loving. She does the job that she is trained to do. She is
reliable, and no matter what else happens during the day,
her relationship with me does not change—as opposed
to people.

"Dottie is not looking out for Dottie's
self-interest. Dottie is looking out for me
in a very devoted way."

MORE PEOPLE I MEET,
ORE I LIKE MY DOG.

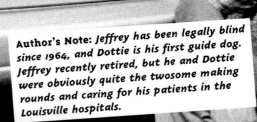

Author's Note: *Jeffrey has been legally blind
since 1964, and Dottie is his first guide dog.
Jeffrey recently retired, but he and Dottie
were obviously quite the twosome making
rounds and caring for his patients in the
Louisville hospitals.*

AGE: 53
EDUCATION: Indiana University Medical School
OCCUPATION: Cardiologist
FAVORITE PASTIMES: Fishing, traveling, music, and computers
FAVORITE BOOK: Books by Tom Clancy
FAVORITE MOVIE: *Forrest Gump* (soundtrack)
PET PEEVE: Government intervention in healthcare

Politically Incorrect
And Proud Of It!

Question Authority
DONNELLY / COLT CUSTOMSTICKERS BOX 188, HAMPTON, CT 06247 (203) 455-9621

THE CAMPAIGN TRAIL
(POLITICS)

IF THE PEOPLE LEAD
THE LEADERS WILL FOLLOW

THE ROAD TO HELL IS PAVED
WITH REPUBLICANS

CLINTON DOESN'T INHALE
HE SUCKS

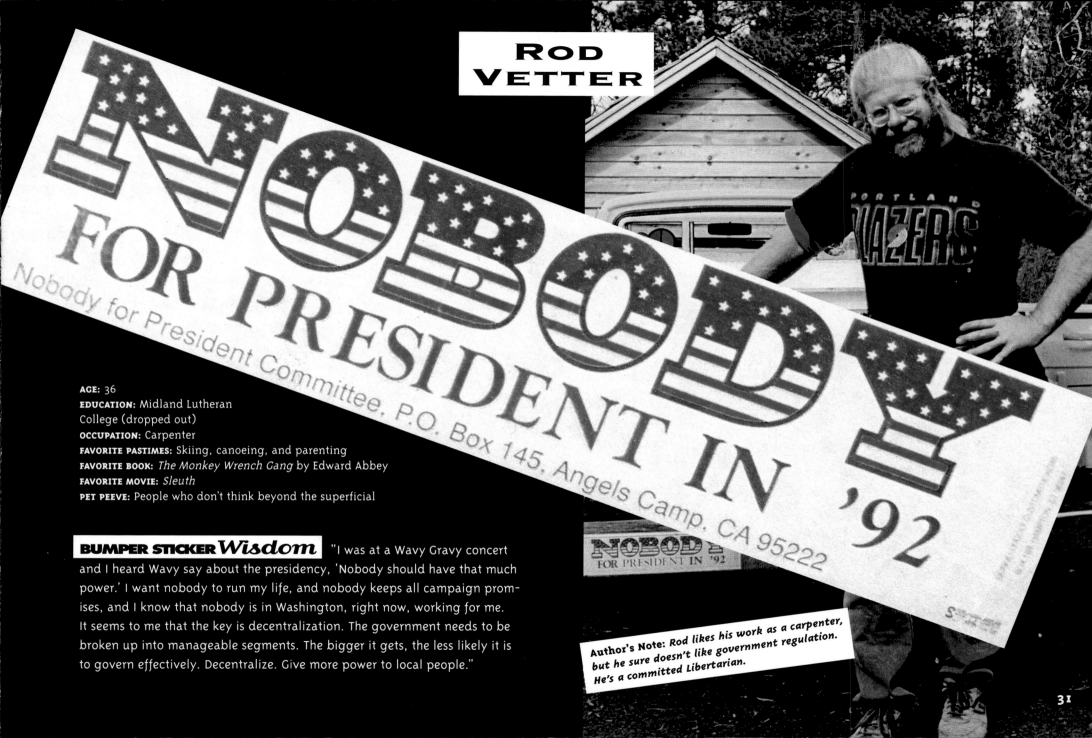

ROD VETTER

NOBODY FOR PRESIDENT IN '92

Nobody for President Committee, P.O. Box 145, Angels Camp, CA 95222

AGE: 36
EDUCATION: Midland Lutheran College (dropped out)
OCCUPATION: Carpenter
FAVORITE PASTIMES: Skiing, canoeing, and parenting
FAVORITE BOOK: *The Monkey Wrench Gang* by Edward Abbey
FAVORITE MOVIE: *Sleuth*
PET PEEVE: People who don't think beyond the superficial

BUMPER STICKER *Wisdom* "I was at a Wavy Gravy concert and I heard Wavy say about the presidency, 'Nobody should have that much power.' I want nobody to run my life, and nobody keeps all campaign promises, and I know that nobody is in Washington, right now, working for me. It seems to me that the key is decentralization. The government needs to be broken up into manageable segments. The bigger it gets, the less likely it is to govern effectively. Decentralize. Give more power to local people."

Author's Note: Rod likes his work as a carpenter, but he sure doesn't like government regulation. He's a committed Libertarian.

31

JON HAGEN

AGE: 57

EDUCATION: Portland State University (historical social sciences)

OCCUPATION: Bookstore owner

FAVORITE PASTIMES: Reading, hiking, swimming, and attending musical events

FAVORITE BOOK: Travel and Northwest history books

FAVORITE MOVIE: Robert Altman films

PET PEEVE: Willful ignorance

BUMPER STICKER *Wisdom*   "During the Reagan years we, those of us who are progressive and liberal, despaired that we would ever see the end of the tunnel. We were afraid that the light we saw at the end of the tunnel was simply another freight train rushing to crush our hopes and programs. So we grasped any small ray of hope we could find, and the bumper sticker was just an expression of hope."

REAGANITIS *

CAN BE CURED !

© OLVERO 1987   Olvero PO Box 14265 Portland, OR 97214   * Another social disease!

VOTE DEMOCRAT

MIKE MARTIN

Author's Note: In the interview, Mike clarified his criticism, essentially that Bush had ignored the domestic economy. Mike's bumper sticker was one of the few I saw in which the meaning reversed as you got closer to it. From afar it looked like a "Bush" bumper sticker. However, as you approached, "Bush" became "Bullshit," which was really the message Mike wanted to convey.

AGE: 47

EDUCATION: Orange Coast College (police science)

OCCUPATION: Commercial fisherman

FAVORITE PASTIMES: Driving in the woods and getting away from the city

FAVORITE BOOK: *Cannery Row* by John Steinbeck

FAVORITE MOVIE: *The Hustler*

PET PEEVE: Television preachers

BUMPER STICKER *Wisdom* "I bought the bumper sticker before the election. What it means is what it looks like. Bush's bullshit was, 'It's the economy, stupid.' He was just a wishy-washy guy."

K.D. "SNAKE" SHOOK

AGE: 50
EDUCATION: Oklahoma State University (football)
OCCUPATION: Retired operator of a high-pressure welding company; also a cop, plumber, and licensed electrician
FAVORITE PASTIMES: Snake hunting and fishing
FAVORITE BOOK: Poetry by Alice Spawn Newton
FAVORITE MOVIE: John Wayne movies
PET PEEVE: Liars, cheats, and stealers

BUMPER STICKER *Wisdom* "My cousin started this bumper sticker. He's a minister in Wichita, Kansas, and

I'm one of the 60 percent that didn't vote for Bill Clinton. Bill Clinton was elected by electoral vote, and I don't think the people knew what they were getting. I display this bumper sticker proudly."

I AM ONE OF THE 60% WHO DID NOT VOTE FOR BILL CLINTON

MORRIS KEUDELL

AGE: 51
EDUCATION: St. Helens High School and real-estate school
OCCUPATION: Sales and public relations for Silverado Horse and Stock Trailers
FAVORITE PASTIMES: Filling a cooler with cold beer and exploring the back roads
FAVORITE BOOK: *The Last of the Pioneers* by Rick Steber
FAVORITE MOVIE: *Dances with Wolves*
PET PEEVE: People who drive RVs and don't drive the speed limit

BUMPER STICKER *Wisdom* "My insurance agent gave me this bumper sticker. It's been on my pickup over a year and I have not had one person say a derogatory thing about it. Not one.

FIRST HILLARY, THEN GENNIFER, NOW US!

"I have people going by me and giving me the high sign and agreeing. I had a lady stop me last Christmas. She said if she could find one for her husband she'd pay $100. She said he'd love it for Christmas.

"I can hardly wait for an election."

FIRST HILLARY,
THEN GENNIFER,
NOW US!

Author's Note: Can you imagine a town called Bucksnort, Tennessee? That's where I met Bill.

AGE: 80
EDUCATION: Wolfcreek Grammar School
OCCUPATION: Ex-moonshiner and U.S. Army survivor of the Battle of the Bulge
FAVORITE PASTIMES: Fishing
FAVORITE BOOK: Battle of the Bulge and Civil War books
FAVORITE MOVIE: *Gone with the Wind*
PET PEEVE: "The preacher trying to get me to go to church"

BILL BLACKWELL

BUMPER STICKER *Wisdom* "The 'Wallace for president' bumper sticker was a gift. A fellow that owned a farm not too far from me was Wallace's campaign manager. He gave me this stuff.

"I voted for George Wallace every time he run. I'm a Democrat. I split my ticket 'cause I seen he was there for the people down South.

"My grandfather was a Confederate soldier. He was captured twice. He was in prison when the war ended.

"I felt my feelings for the Confederacy. That's about all I can say, because I've had a tough life, lady."

WALLACE FOR PRESIDENT

RICHARD DOWELL

AGE: 52
EDUCATION: Vernonia Grade School
OCCUPATION: Lumber-mill worker
FAVORITE PASTIMES: Hunting and fishing
FAVORITE MOVIE: *The Cowboys*
PET PEEVE: The IRS

BUMPER STICKER *Wisdom* "My wife and kids picked up the bumper sticker a long time ago and gave it to me. I've had it more than 20 years and have peeled it off one car and put it on my camper.

"I don't think too many people like the IRS. When I pull into a shopping center a lot of people smile and ask me where I bought the bumper sticker.

"I really like the way you followed me off the freeway, then flagged me over. When you asked if you could photograph me and my bumper sticker, I thought, 'Oh boy, that's a strange one.'"

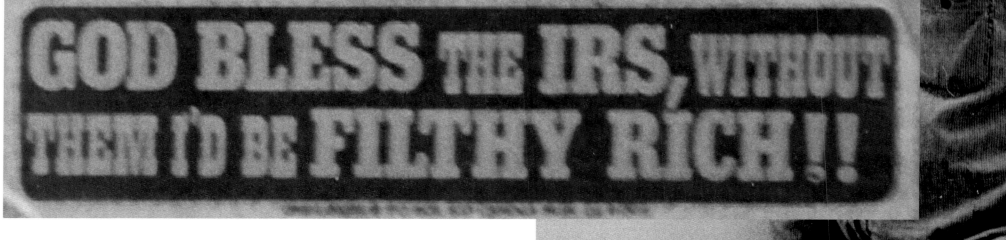

GOD BLESS THE IRS, WITHOUT THEM I'D BE FILTHY RICH!!

HARRY W. SUBLETT

RUSH IS RIGHT!

AGE: 73
EDUCATION: High school in Butler County, Kentucky
OCCUPATION: Retired Chrysler repairman
FAVORITE PASTIMES: Playing bridge, fishing, and driving up and down the road
FAVORITE BOOK: *Shepherd of the Hills* by Harold B. Wright
FAVORITE MOVIE: *The Corn Is Green*
PET PEEVE: The national deficit

BUMPER STICKER *Wisdom*

"Rush Limbaugh has written two books, and they are best-sellers. He puts out a newsletter every month, and he tells you every lie that Clinton tells. Clinton don't like to hear the truth. That's why I like Rush Limbaugh. I listen to him every day. My bumper sticker means Rush is doing the right thing. He's letting the American people know what's going on in Washington—how these politicians are squandering our money. Rush tells the truth, and these politicians don't like to hear the truth."

RUSH IS RIGHT!

AGE: 29
EDUCATION: Brown University (history)
OCCUPATION: Distributor of alternative papers
FAVORITE PASTIMES: Playing pinball, movies, cooking, and reading the alternative press
FAVORITE BOOK: *Even Cowgirls Get the Blues* by Tom Robbins
FAVORITE MOVIE: *The World According to Garp*
PET PEEVE: Portland drivers

BUMPER STICKER *Wisdom* "It's not my favorite bumper sticker, but so many people are so into Rush Limbaugh. I feel like someone needs to say, 'I think he's stupid.' He thinks he's being funny, but he's really just being insulting and narrow-minded. I would want to change the whole capitalist system to a more cooperative system. It's not quite socialist. We'd still have private companies yet with collective ownership. Rush is into individualism, and it breaks down eventually. We live in a society where we have other people around us all the time. Individualism is self-destructive."

JON JACOB

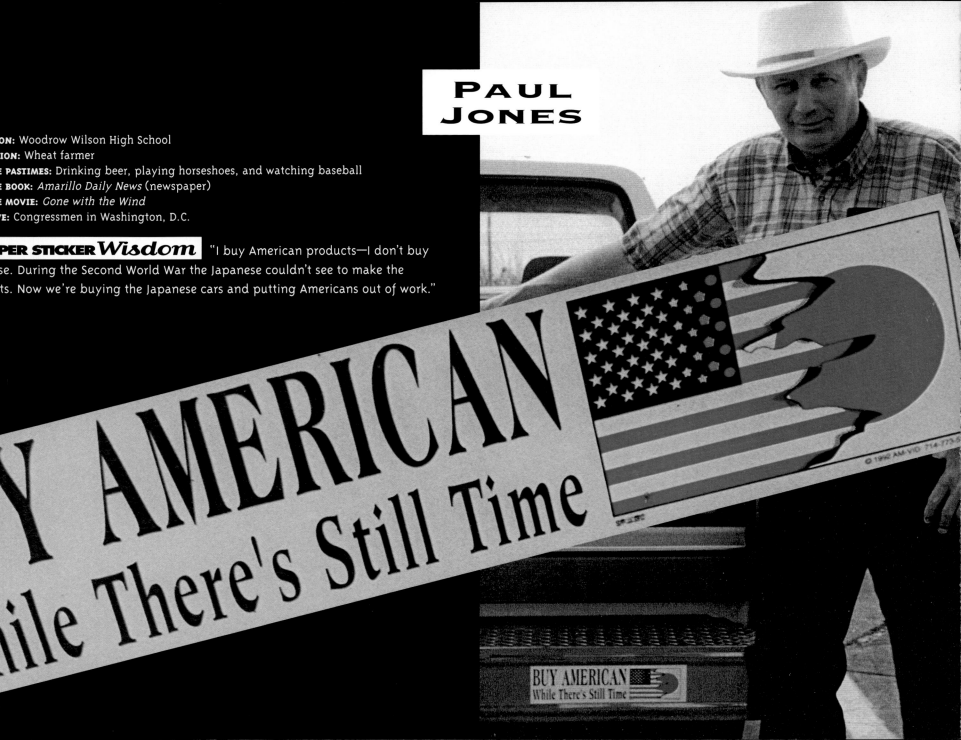

PAUL JONES

AGE: 62
EDUCATION: Woodrow Wilson High School
OCCUPATION: Wheat farmer
FAVORITE PASTIMES: Drinking beer, playing horseshoes, and watching baseball
FAVORITE BOOK: *Amarillo Daily News* (newspaper)
FAVORITE MOVIE: *Gone with the Wind*
PET PEEVE: Congressmen in Washington, D.C.

BUMPER STICKER Wisdom "I buy American products—I don't buy Japanese. During the Second World War the Japanese couldn't see to make the products. Now we're buying the Japanese cars and putting Americans out of work."

BUY AMERICAN
While There's Still Time

"The leader behind the whole deal is David Rockefeller. He is chairman emeritus of the Trilateral group. He is also at the Council on Foreign Relations. Anytime you vote for president or a congressman now, you'll see, if you get to know who's who, they are either members of the Council on Foreign Relations or the Trilateral group. It doesn't matter which party, that's all we've got in. T.H.R.O. means 'Throw the rascals out.'"

T.H.R.O. CONGRESS OUT!
A DISTRESSED CITIZEN

To Reorder Write: T.H.R.O., 4127 West Cypress St., Tampa, FL 33607

T.H.R.O. CONGRESS OUT!
A DISTRESSED CITIZEN

AGE: 80
EDUCATION: University of Depaw (nursing)
OCCUPATION: Retired registered nurse
FAVORITE PASTIMES: Square dancing
FAVORITE BOOK: The Bible
FAVORITE MOVIE: *The Sound of Music*
PET PEEVE: "I'm easygoing."

TROY LORCH

MARILYN BROWER

AGE: 48
EDUCATION: University of Idaho (education and history, working on a master's)
OCCUPATION: Owner (with her husband) of a general store in Clayton, Idaho
FAVORITE PASTIMES: Horseback riding, hiking, hunting, fishing, and reading
FAVORITE BOOK: *After the War Was Over: Hanoi and Saigon* by Neil Sheehan and *Or I'll Dress You in Mourning* by Larry Collins and Dominique Lapierre
FAVORITE MOVIE: *Out of Africa* and *Lawrence of Arabia*
PET PEEVE: Men who hate women

"If We Can't Reform It, We Will Overthrow It!"

Author's Note: In our interview, Marilyn told me that she had been wooed by a militia group, but she found it too extreme for her tastes.

She also added that their general store in Clayton, Idaho, is a watering hole for a cross-section of people and that most of their customers see her bumper sticker, laugh, and say, "Right on."

BUMPER STICKER *Wisdom*

"What prompted this bumper sticker was the federal injunction that came down to tie up all the logging, mining, and ranching in this country. The frustration is that our government is so corrupt. The regulations are in our face. They are stupid. We can't work with them as common working people. The government tells us we can't log, we can't mine, and cattlemen can't turn their cattle out. People are upset and angry.

"Americans need to realize that most people are good. There are more good people than bad.

"People here are tired of taxes; they're tired of stupidity; and American people aren't stupid."

AGE: 53
EDUCATION: San Diego City College (acoustic engineering)
OCCUPATION: Magician
FAVORITE PASTIMES: "We live, eat, and sleep magic." Also traveling
FAVORITE BOOK: Tarzan books by Edgar Rice Burroughs
FAVORITE MOVIE: *Forrest Gump* and *Play It Again, Sam*
PET PEEVE: Local government intervention in individual rights

DAVID EMERY

BUMPER STICKER *Wisdom* "I was thumbing through a rack of bumper stickers when I saw 'Great leaders are rare, so I'm following myself.' It was the only time I've seen this bumper sticker.

"I'm not impressed by great leaders. I've been a Republican the greater part of my adult life, and there is not a Republican I would have voted for on the ticket. George Bush was no good. I think Bill Clinton is lousy.

"I voted for Ross Perot. I think, there is a man who has done precisely what needs to be done with this country. Grab the bull by the horns and go do what has got to be done. If he were campaigning again, I would help the man campaign.

GREAT LEADERS ARE RARE, SO I'M FOLLOWING MYSELF

© 85 J&P Products

"I just don't want to be someone's pawn. I'm known as a hustler. I go out there and create a want. My feelings are, I can't work for anybody else. I go to work for people, and I hate to say this, but about 50 percent of the time I look upon them as being total idiots. They are stupid. I have not worked for another company for many, many years. The last job I had, I got fired for telling the boss he was an idiot."

MAGIC IS A VANISHING ART

43

I HATE
SLOW CARS IN
THE FAST LANE
© 85 J&P Products

If You Can Read This
You're TOO DAMN CLOSE!

IF YOU GET ANY CLOSER,
I'LL FART

BUMPER TO
BUMPER
(TRAFFIC)

It's bad enough driving sober.
Don't drive drunk.
PHRESH STICKERS (503) 285-6539

IF YOU DRINK LIKE A FISH
SWIM, DON'T DRIVE

0-55 MPH IN 11 MINUTES

AGE: 45

EDUCATION: Portland State University (psychology)

OCCUPATION: Formerly in financial services; currently pursuing an art career

FAVORITE PASTIMES: Horses, cars, hiking, skiing, and "playing with my llama named Johnny Unitas and spending time with my husband and daughters"

FAVORITE BOOK: *Hanta Yo* by Ruth Beebe Hill

FAVORITE MOVIE: *Dances with Wolves*

PET PEEVE: Rude drivers, call waiting, and hearing *Porsche* pronounced with one syllable

BUMPER STICKER *Wisdom* "About my bumper sticker: We collect classic cars, and I'd always wanted a little Nash Metropolitan convertible. My husband bought this one as a gift for me. We named her 'Kippy.' She came with this bumper sticker, and it's too cute to remove. She does boast a 52-horsepower engine! With or without her sticker, she causes a lot of smiles when we drive her."

JEANNIE GRETZ

JOHN SHEFLER

AGE: 67
EDUCATION: Washington State University (master's in education)
OCCUPATION: Retired industrial-education teacher
FAVORITE PASTIMES: Square dancing, RV-ing, and woodworking
FAVORITE BOOK: *National Geographic* magazine
FAVORITE MOVIE: *Forrest Gump* and *The Bridge on the River Kwai*
PET PEEVE: People with four-letter-word bumper stickers and telephone solicitors

BUMPER STICKER *Wisdom* "I saw this bumper sticker down at the beach, and I have always said that I just didn't think that I wanted to put a bumper sticker on my car. But I don't know why,

So many PEDESTRIANS ...so little time

when I saw 'So many pedestrians . . . so little time,' it just said, 'John, you've got to buy this and put it on your car.'
"It's been fun having it on there. I can't explain it."

So many PEDESTRIANS
...so little time

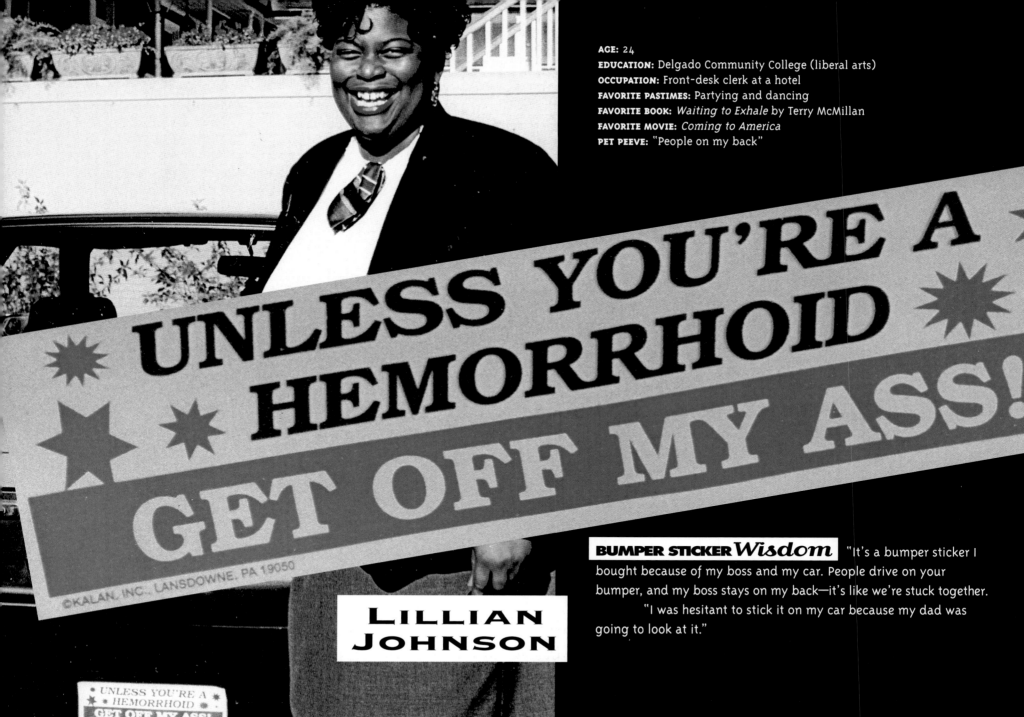

AGE: 24
EDUCATION: Delgado Community College (liberal arts)
OCCUPATION: Front-desk clerk at a hotel
FAVORITE PASTIMES: Partying and dancing
FAVORITE BOOK: *Waiting to Exhale* by Terry McMillan
FAVORITE MOVIE: *Coming to America*
PET PEEVE: "People on my back"

UNLESS YOU'RE A HEMORRHOID
GET OFF MY ASS!

©KALAN, INC., LANSDOWNE, PA 19050

LILLIAN JOHNSON

BUMPER STICKER *Wisdom* "It's a bumper sticker I bought because of my boss and my car. People drive on your bumper, and my boss stays on my back—it's like we're stuck together.

"I was hesitant to stick it on my car because my dad was going to look at it."

UNLESS YOU'RE A
HEMORRHOID
GET OFF MY ASS!

AGE: 42
EDUCATION: Franklin College (liberal arts)
OCCUPATION: CEO of the Macheezmo Mouse restaurant chain
FAVORITE PASTIMES: "Spending time with my children"
FAVORITE BOOK: *All the Pretty Horses* by Cormac McCarthy
FAVORITE MOVIE: *Dr. Strangelove*
PET PEEVE: Divorce lawyers

BUMPER STICKER *Wisdom* "I have to scroll the clock back to about six or seven years ago when I got the bumper sticker. At the time I was building a restaurant in downtown Portland. Through the process of building the restaurant, we were the recipients of an inordinate number of parking tickets. Anyway, we were getting a ton of tickets, and we started papering the window with parking tickets, and it was becoming very hostile. I was in San Francisco for the weekend and I saw the bumper sticker, and I bought two of them, one of which I put on my red Jeep. The metermaids immediately saw my bumper sticker and took such offense to it. They would actually wait to get me. This was now war. The gauntlet had been thrown down. The day we actually opened the restaurant, here I was, the president and founder of the company, having my car towed away because of so many unpaid parking tickets and this big battle going on, probably as a result of this bumper sticker. The reason I have the bumper sticker is I feel as though it is somewhat

TIGER WARREN

METERMAIDS EAT THEIR YOUNG

METERMAIDS EAT THEIR YOUNG

true.
And it is probably sexist. It would be *meterpersons* now. Meterpersons are just plain mean people. They don't like people. Meterpersons have no mercy."

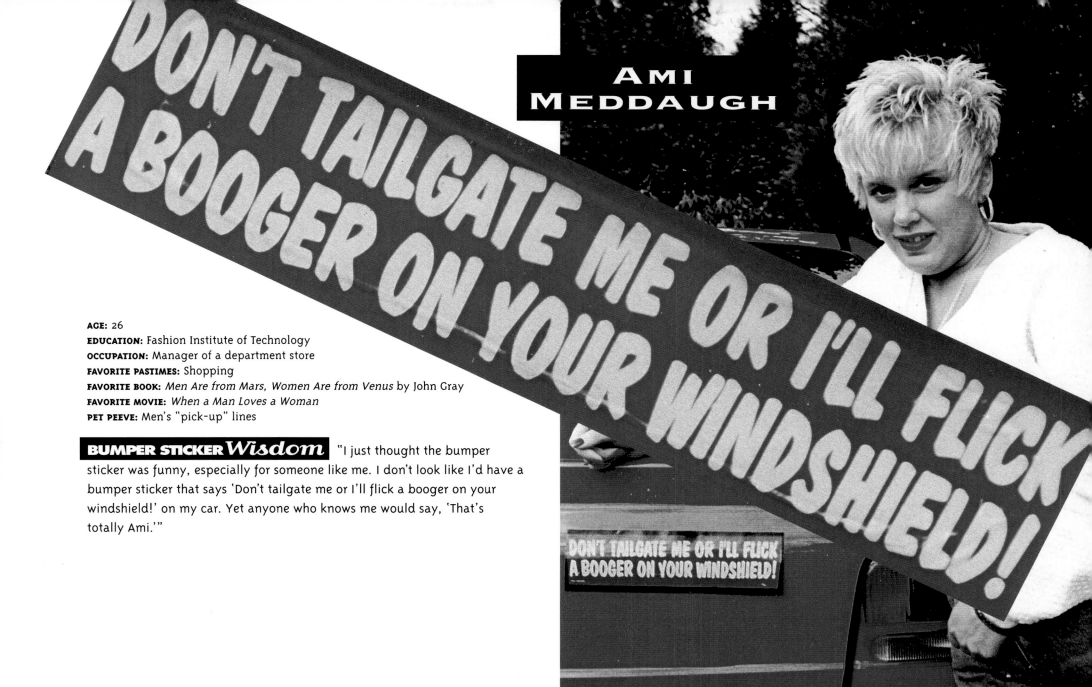

AMI MEDDAUGH

AGE: 26
EDUCATION: Fashion Institute of Technology
OCCUPATION: Manager of a department store
FAVORITE PASTIMES: Shopping
FAVORITE BOOK: *Men Are from Mars, Women Are from Venus* by John Gray
FAVORITE MOVIE: *When a Man Loves a Woman*
PET PEEVE: Men's "pick-up" lines

BUMPER STICKER *Wisdom* "I just thought the bumper sticker was funny, especially for someone like me. I don't look like I'd have a bumper sticker that says 'Don't tailgate me or I'll flick a booger on your windshield!' on my car. Yet anyone who knows me would say, 'That's totally Ami.'"

DON'T TAILGATE ME OR I'LL FLICK A BOOGER ON YOUR WINDSHIELD!

49

AGE: 43
EDUCATION: Melrose High School
OCCUPATION: Security officer
FAVORITE PASTIMES: Basketball, horseback riding, fishing, and hunting
FAVORITE MOVIE: *Dirty Harry*
PET PEEVE: People who drive too slow in the left lane on the expressway

Author's Note: I originally stopped Grady when I saw his other bumper sticker that read "Titty bingo." This truly made me wonder, what does this mean? It turns out to be a game from a radio station in Tennessee using bra sizes, but Grady had it on his car simply because he likes the sound of the words. Enough questions asked on that one.

Wreck drunk driving before it WRECKS you.

THE MED ELVIS PRESLEY MEMORIAL TRAUMA CENTER

BUMPER STICKER *Wisdom* "This is a sticker from where I work, the Regional Medical Center in Memphis. At the Trauma Center I see people come in all the time when they've been hit by drunk drivers.

"We had a lady at my job—she was on her way from work and this drunk driver hit her. Right now she's paralyzed from the waist down. It's an awful situation to see her come in for treatment when that could have been avoided. This guy had been drinking and ran several red lights and hit her. Now her husband has to suffer as well as her kids.

"It's a nationwide problem and a grave situation."

titty bingo
Rock-n-Roll

AGE: 37
EDUCATION: International Air Academy
OCCUPATION: Nursery worker
FAVORITE PASTIMES: Sewing, crafts, travel, boating, and shopping
FAVORITE BOOK: *McCall's* magazine
FAVORITE MOVIE: *Scent of a Woman*
PET PEEVE: People who are impatient

KAREN JORGENSEN

BUMPER STICKER *Wisdom* "Stephanie's death was devastating to our entire family. I would like to get the message across to make people stop and think so other families don't have to go through the same pain.

"The boy who was responsible still drinks and drives. He is still carrying on the same way as before this happened.

"If people could only know the feelings that the families experience after they lose someone [Stephanie had a two-year-old daughter at the time of the crash], they would probably never do it again. If I could only let them know how bad it hurts, they would never drink and drive.

"One day a repairman asked me, 'Doesn't that bumper sticker bother you when you get in the car every day? I would think it would depress you and make you think of it all over again.' I told him that it's on my mind all the time anyway. It doesn't matter whether I see the bumper sticker or not. It matters that others see it. It is something I can never forget. It's like I want to go out there and scream, 'Please don't do this!'"

A DRUNK DRIVER KILLED MY DAUGHTER

WOMEN are Natural Leaders
YOU'RE FOLLOWING ONE NOW!

Sex is like pizza!
Even when it's bad it's kinda good.

UPPITY WOMEN UNITE

CRUISE
CONTROL
(MEN, WOMEN, AND RELATIONSHIPS)

REAL MEN
DON'T USE PORN

Women have to be in the mood.
Men just have to be in the room.

I STILL MISS MY "EX"
But My Aim is Improving

CAUTION! I can go from 0 to BITCH in 2.5 seconds

AGE: 33
EDUCATION: La Grande High School
OCCUPATION: Bartender
FAVORITE PASTIMES: Spending money
FAVORITE BOOK: *Every Living Thing* by James Heriot
FAVORITE MOVIE: *Under Siege*

BUMPER STICKER *Wisdom* "A friend at work gave me these. My family says it applies sometimes."

DEBBIE SPOELSTRA

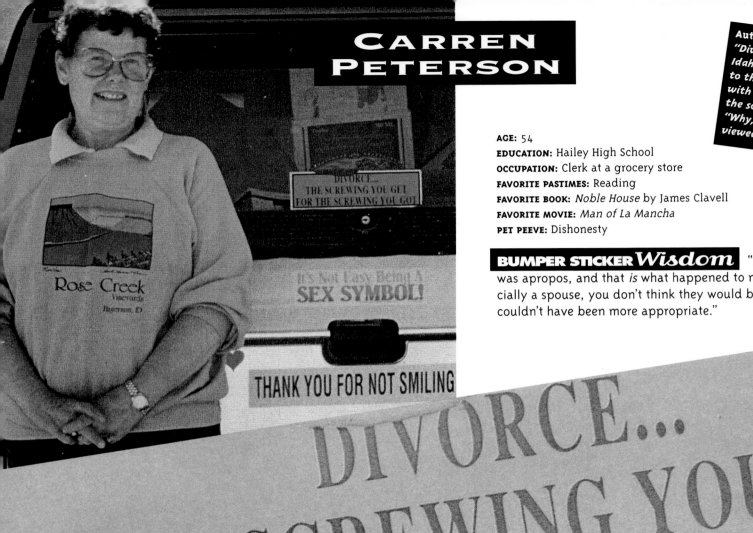

CARREN PETERSON

AGE: 54

EDUCATION: Hailey High School

OCCUPATION: Clerk at a grocery store

FAVORITE PASTIMES: Reading

FAVORITE BOOK: *Noble House* by James Clavell

FAVORITE MOVIE: *Man of La Mancha*

PET PEEVE: Dishonesty

Author's Note: When I entered Guffy's Market to inquire about the "Divorce" bumper sticker, it seemed like the entire town of Carey, Idaho, was there doing their weekly shopping. I bashfully whispered to the clerk behind the cash register, "Do you know who owns a truck with a bumper sticker that says 'Divorce . . . the screwing you get for the screwing you got'?" She looked up at me, grinned, and said, "Why, I do, dearie." Carren was one of the sweetest people I interviewed, but she sure had strong opinions about her ex-husband.

BUMPER STICKER *Wisdom* "I bought the bumper sticker because at the time it was apropos, and that *is* what happened to me! I was married for 26 years and, you know, especially a spouse, you don't think they would be dishonest. If I'd made up the words myself, I couldn't have been more appropriate."

DIVORCE...
THE SCREWING YOU GET
FOR THE SCREWING YOU GOT

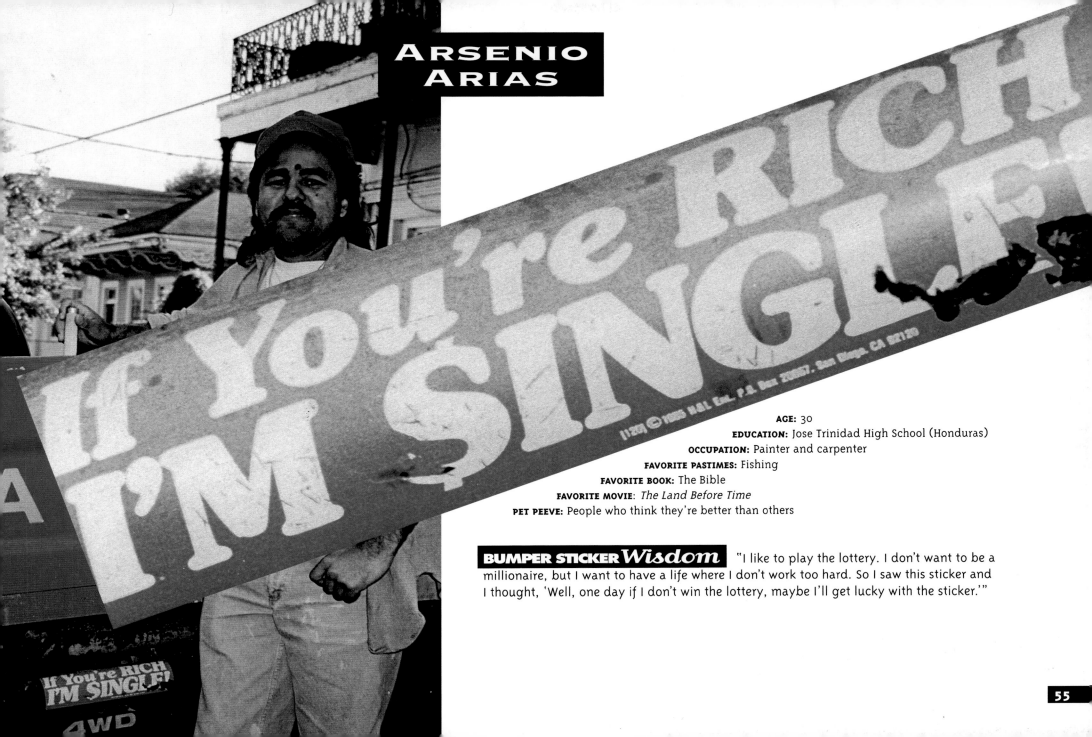

ARSENIO ARIAS

AGE: 30
EDUCATION: Jose Trinidad High School (Honduras)
OCCUPATION: Painter and carpenter
FAVORITE PASTIMES: Fishing
FAVORITE BOOK: The Bible
FAVORITE MOVIE: *The Land Before Time*
PET PEEVE: People who think they're better than others

BUMPER STICKER *Wisdom* "I like to play the lottery. I don't want to be a millionaire, but I want to have a life where I don't work too hard. So I saw this sticker and I thought, 'Well, one day if I don't win the lottery, maybe I'll get lucky with the sticker.'"

AGE: 23
EDUCATION: Phagans' Beauty Schools
OCCUPATION: Student
FAVORITE PASTIMES: Playing in a heavy-metal band
FAVORITE BOOK: Batman comics
FAVORITE MOVIE: *The Kentucky Fried Movie*
PET PEEVE: Hypocrites

JOHN RINKER

BUMPER STICKER Wisdom "Why did I buy it? Because, well, just take a look at my car. Girls drive by and give me a thumbs-up sign. People laugh at it."

Author's Note: *I was a little nervous at first when I asked John about his bumper sticker. He told me about not being rich, but I don't think he was comfortable commenting on the second half of the message. This bumper sticker, like many others, was motivated by humor.*

WHY CAN'T I BE RICH INSTEAD OF WELL HUNG!

SKU #675868

PLANET EARTH GRAPHICS, INC., BOSTON, MA.

KATY VAN DIS

AGE: 19
EDUCATION: Washington State University (environmental science)
OCCUPATION: Student
FAVORITE PASTIMES: Exercise, hiking, biking, camping, and having fun
FAVORITE MOVIE: *Bean Trees* by Barbara Kingsolver
FAVORITE MOVIE: *Dances with Wolves*
PET PEEVE: None

BUMPER STICKER *Wisdom* "Actually, I didn't buy the bumper sticker. My boyfriend bought it and left it in my car. So when I got home I said, What is this?! I decided that if he was going to buy it for me. I might as well put it on my car to show everybody I can do this. I'm standing up for myself and just saying, hey, I'm not the only one."

SMALL-BUSTED WOMEN HAVE BIG HEARTS

J. BOYER

AGE: 36
EDUCATION: Hillsboro High School
OCCUPATION: Aircraft serviceperson
FAVORITE PASTIMES: Women-watching
FAVORITE BOOK: *Nothing Down* by Robert G. Allen
FAVORITE MOVIE: *Summer Lovers*
PET PEEVE: Unkept promises

BUMPER STICKER *Wisdom* "This sticker means there is just not enough time to enjoy all the beautiful women that there are in the world. To be honest, well, I have, let's see, one, two, four girlfriends—plus my wife. By the way, my wife, Robbyn, gave me the bumper sticker."

SO MANY WOMEN SO LITTLE TIME

SO MANY WOMEN
SO LITTLE TIME

Author's Note: *Appropriately enough, I met J. Boyer on Valentine's Day as he was gathering balloons and flowers for his "friends."*

So Many Boys So Few Men!

EARTH GRAPHICS • 80 ASHFORD STREET, ALLSTON, MA 02134

AGE: 42
EDUCATION: State University of New York College at Binghamton
OCCUPATION: Construction contractor
FAVORITE PASTIMES: Motorcycles and camping
FAVORITE BOOK: *Brothers Karamazov* by Fyodor Dostovesky
FAVORITE MOVIE: *Rocky*
PET PEEVE: The subject of this bumper sticker

BUMPER STICKER *Wisdom* "The irresponsibility of men is just an obnoxious development in our history. The scores of women who are left with children without their dads, I think, is a really terrible thing. There are children who have been radically hurt by a man who said, 'Hey, I think I'd rather be with *her* than my wife'—well, no shit—isn't that understood? But then again, *she* is the same age as his daughter.

"My wife has her master's in social work and deals with these kids who don't have dads. They have no security, no stability. I think this situation is a bad reflection on all men. Today mature men are so rare."

So Many Boys
So Few Men!

CHRIS CAPWELL

59

BUMPER STICKER Wisdom "Basically I just liked the bumper sticker. I thought it was funny. Life is too short.

"As far as 'ugly men,' I don't see people as ugly or beautiful as far as appearance. Ugly comes from the inside. I've known people who I thought were beautiful when I first met them, but when I got to know them better, they turned out to be ugly—

DENISE WILSON

LIFE IS TOO SHORT TO DATE UGLY MEN

©STICKER ART SA423

I've been married four times. My other bumper sticker also relates to life: 'Don't take life too seriously, it isn't permanent.'"

AGE: 42
EDUCATION: Dublin High School
OCCUPATION: Customer-service representative
FAVORITE PASTIMES: Roller-skating, dancing, swimming, and "all kinds of things"
FAVORITE BOOK: Books by Erma Bombeck
FAVORITE MOVIE: *Defending Your Life*
PET PEEVE: Ignorance

MAGGIE HALFORD

AGE: 28
EDUCATION: Portland Community College (jewelry)
OCCUPATION: Goldsmith
FAVORITE PASTIMES: Team penning with my quarter horse paint gelding
FAVORITE BOOK: *The Cat Who* series by Lilian Jackson Braun
FAVORITE MOVIE: *Pure Country*
PET PEEVE: Dishonesty

BUMPER STICKER *Wisdom* "I put the bumper sticker on my truck when I was in a disagreement with a fellow I was going out with. It had been an ongoing nightmare over a couple of years. He had been seeing someone else and I just felt jilted. I was so angry. I slapped that sucker [bumper sticker] on, and it's been on my truck ever since.

"I kinda date one other fellow now, and he is just a sweetheart, so I think I've got to take the bumper sticker off. He's never said anything about it."

THE MORE I KNOW MEN The More I Like My Dog!

THE MORE I KNOW MEN
The More I Like My Dog!
COUNTRY

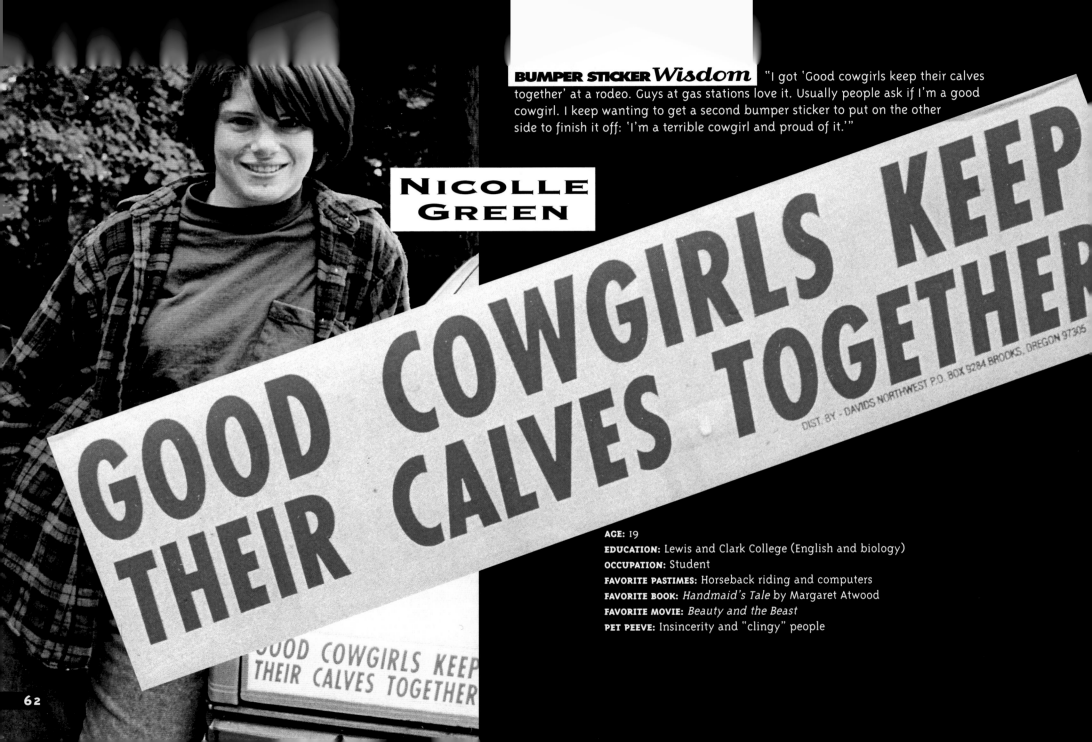

"I got 'Good cowgirls keep their calves together' at a rodeo. Guys at gas stations love it. Usually people ask if I'm a good cowgirl. I keep wanting to get a second bumper sticker to put on the other side to finish it off: 'I'm a terrible cowgirl and proud of it.'"

NICOLLE GREEN

GOOD COWGIRLS KEEP THEIR CALVES TOGETHER

DIST. BY - DAVIDS NORTHWEST P.O. BOX 9284 BROOKS, OREGON 97305

AGE: 19
EDUCATION: Lewis and Clark College (English and biology)
OCCUPATION: Student
FAVORITE PASTIMES: Horseback riding and computers
FAVORITE BOOK: *Handmaid's Tale* by Margaret Atwood
FAVORITE MOVIE: *Beauty and the Beast*
PET PEEVE: Insincerity and "clingy" people

GOOD COWGIRLS KEEP THEIR CALVES TOGETHER

"When I got the bumper sticker I was at a rodeo and I met this guy. His name is David. He's a bull-rider, and he's got this butt, and, well, it would drive anybody nuts."

JENNIE FOSTER

Author's Note: I met Jennie at the annual Mosquito Festival in Paisley, Oregon. She really is 14, and she put the bumper sticker on her mother's truck.

WRANGLER BUTTS DRIVE ME NUTS

DIST. BY - DAVIDS NORTHWEST P.O. BOX 9284 BROOKS, OREGON 97305

WRANGLER BUTTS DRIVE ME NUTS

AGE: 14
EDUCATION: Monroe High School
OCCUPATION: Student
FAVORITE PASTIMES: Riding horses and looking for cowboys
FAVORITE BOOK: *Horse & Rider* magazine
FAVORITE MOVIE: *8 Seconds*
PET PEEVE: Cowboys who wear baggy Wranglers

"Basically I bought this bumper sticker because I own a houseboat on a lake. I go to the houseboat all the time and fish a lot. It's more for a joke than anything. My wife gets a kick out of it, and other truck drivers ask me a lot about fishing. They ask me where I got it and say it's what they need."

JAMES ROBERTSON

AGE: 49
EDUCATION: Fort Smith High School
OCCUPATION: Truck driver
FAVORITE PASTIMES: Fishing and boating
FAVORITE BOOK: Car magazines
FAVORITE MOVIE: *The Beverly Hillbillies*
PET PEEVE: People who cut you off the road

MY WIFE SAID IF I DON'T QUIT FISHING SHE IS GOING TO DIVORCE ME GOD I'M GOING TO MISS HER

LINDYCAL® P.O. BOX 4322 • SARASOTA, FL 34230-4322

Author's Note: *James was on his way to California when I followed him off the freeway to a truck stop in Texas. His wife and his dog, Shadow, were with him—hence, my deduction that he and his wife have come to an understanding about his fishing.*

LYLA FOGGIA

AGE: 48

EDUCATION: University of Washington

OCCUPATION: Author of *Reel Women: The World of Women Who Fish* and former West Coast vice president of publicity for Tri-Star Pictures

FAVORITE PASTIMES: Reading, fly fishing, and mushrooming

FAVORITE BOOK: *Molly Ivins Can't Say That, Can She?* by Molly Ivins

FAVORITE MOVIE: *Terms of Endearment* and *The Conformist*

PET PEEVE: "Litter and garbage dumped in our national forests"

BUMPER STICKER *Wisdom*

"I've fished my entire life. In 1988 I moved to a house that is on a steelhead river, and suddenly I was getting to live the kind of dream that I thought would come true only after retirement. I can get up early and grab my rod and go out there for an hour or two before work, or I can take a break through the day and go out on the river for ten minutes. I am passionate about fishing.

"One day it suddenly occurred to me that I wanted to write about other women who fish. This book has sections about women fly fishing, bass fishing, big-game angling, and then there is a section on women in the industry.

"Men have been some of the most valuable resources I've had in this book. Furthermore, I had a guy at Northwest Steelheaders' Association tell me that within their 2,000-member organization, the men whose wives and girlfriends fish with them are the most envied. A lot of the women in the book were, or are, married to great anglers.

"I don't use the word *fisherman*. In the fly-fishing world, now you often see the word *fly fisher*. I use the word *angler*. Mind you, a lot of women don't mind being called *fishermen*. It's not a big raging issue. Everybody hates the word *fisherperson*. The women who make a living fishing call themselves *pro-anglers*.

"Nearly 19 million women fish. One-third of all anglers are women—believe it or not."

DIANA KAISER

AGE: 36
EDUCATION: Franklin College (Lugano, Switzerland)
OCCUPATION: Hotel public-relations director at Loews L'enfant in Washington, D.C.
FAVORITE PASTIMES: Singing, tennis, sailing, and fund-raising for the Humane Society
FAVORITE BOOK: *A Book of Angels* by Sophy Burnham
FAVORITE MOVIE: *Now, Voyager*
PET PEEVE: People who don't follow through on promises

BUMPER STICKER *Wisdom* "Actually, a friend gave me this bumper sticker. She thought it would be perfect for me because I'm always out, I'm always happy, and I'm always doing things—going to parties or working on projects or playing tennis or sailing. I kind of never get down, and I exercise a lot and I'm always happy. I guess sometimes I act a little wild. I've had couriers on bicycles say, 'Yeah, I love that bumper sticker.' People just get a kick out of it. Being in the hotel business, there is a bumper sticker I'm dying to get that says 'Free Leona.' Not that I want her free; I just think it's totally hysterical."

WILD WOMEN don't get the blues

NORTHERN SUN MERCHANDISING 2916 E. LAKE, MPLS. M.N. 55406 (612) 729-2001

WILD WOMEN
don't get the blues

SHOSHANNA AHART

AGE: 31
EDUCATION: American University (MFA)
OCCUPATION: Artist and painter
FAVORITE PASTIMES: Going to museums, theater, and sailing
FAVORITE BOOK: *The Mists of Avalon* by Marion Zimmer Bradley
FAVORITE MOVIE: Prefers live theater: *The Skin of Our Teeth* by Thornton Wilder
PET PEEVE: People who assume artists and blondes are unorganized and "ditzy"

BUMPER STICKER *Wisdom* "The reason I bought the bumper sticker is I feel that a woman doesn't need a man to be a complete person, and too many women don't adhere to that or don't believe that. So I saw this bumper sticker and I thought, aha, I'm going to put this on my car. I think it's very important for people to be complete individuals within themselves. I don't have any problems with having a relationship with a man, but I feel it should be something you want to have and it should be an addition to you. Women tend to

A WOMAN WITHOUT A MAN IS LIKE A FISH WITHOUT A BICYCLE

think the bumper
sticker is humorous, and they like it. I think men get
really intimidated. This is a personal litmus test I have with the men I've gone out with. If they say something negative about the bumper sticker or if they don't think it's funny at all—I've actually had this happen more than not—then I have a tendency to feel that they're not really the type of person I want to be around. Some men feel really threatened and get all uppity and defensive. One guy got in a big argument with me. That was the end of him."

67

JIM BENNETT

AGE: 48
EDUCATION: University of New Mexico (philosophy)
OCCUPATION: Carpenter
FAVORITE PASTIMES: Hiking and motorcycle riding
FAVORITE BOOK: *On the Road* by Jack Kerouac
FAVORITE MOVIE: *Yellow Submarine*
PET PEEVE: Martyrs

DON'T STARE AT MY THING

BUMPER STICKER *Wisdom* "My car is a Volkswagen 'Thing.' When 'The Thing' came out in the '60s, we thought they were ugly and weird, and they cost $500 more than a 'Beetle.' Who would want a ragtop, ugly-looking 'Thing'? I like the name, 'The Thing,' because people say, 'What is that thing?'

"The bumper sticker came from a trim shop in Arizona. They sent it when I bought a box of parts. I loved it when I saw it.

"The most memorable reaction to 'Don't stare at my thing' is that I've had girls try to pull me over on the freeway."

AGE: 41

EDUCATION: Berkley Business School
OCCUPATION: Food-service supervision for a school district
FAVORITE PASTIMES: Spending money
FAVORITE BOOK: Books by Sidney Sheldon and Mary Higgins Clark
FAVORITE MOVIE: *The Godfather*
PET PEEVE: Penny-pinchers

FEEL SAFE TONIGHT SLEEP WITH A COP

BUMPER STICKER *Wisdom* "People know my husband is with the New York Police Department because my license plate is F.O.P., which is the Fraternal Order of Police, and they connect my bumper sticker to my license. My husband brought the bumper sticker home to me, and I do feel safe at night. When we were first married I was afraid, but not now. He taught me how to shoot a gun, and I have a pistol permit.

"Being married to a cop is a very difficult life. My other bumper sticker should be 'Don't marry a cop.' We've been married 21 years, but the divorce rate for New York City cops is 75 percent. I tell my girls, don't ever marry a cop. I never thought I'd make 21 years. How many times I thought my husband was killed. There was one time he didn't come home for a couple of days, and I prepared myself. I said, 'I think he's dead.' I was ready for the big boss to come knock on my door and tell me, 'Your husband is gone.' My husband is usually the first cop to break down a door. He says, 'If I can save these people, I will.' I guess I don't blame him. It is his job, and it is his love.

"Sometimes I say to my husband, 'You may be a lieutenant at work, but I'm the captain of *this* house.'"

FEEL SAFE TONIGHT
SLEEP WITH A COP

JUDITH S. WINTERS

AGE: 50

EDUCATION: Endicott College, Brown University, and the Rhode Island School of Design

OCCUPATION: Mother and artist

FAVORITE PASTIMES: Gardening and channel-surfing through news programs

FAVORITE BOOK: *Symptoms: The Complete Home Medical Encyclopedia* by Isadore Rosenfeld

FAVORITE MOVIE: *Sophie's Choice*

PET PEEVE: Injustice without a consequence

BUMPER STICKER *Wisdom* "I was very concerned about the qualifications of Clarence Thomas to the Supreme Court before I ever heard of Anita Hill. When she was called before the confirmation hearings and then was treated so badly, I was appalled. I decided I had to do something. I wrote to all the senators who were in attendance at the hearings. I just wanted to record my dissatisfaction.

"Several months later my husband and I were in San Francisco, and I saw a car that had the bumper sticker, 'Anita told the truth.' It was the only bumper sticker I had ever seen that I really coveted.

"As I was pressing the bumper sticker on my car I realized that this was risk-taking. There were going to be consequences to this bumper sticker. It wasn't like a bumper sticker that says

ANITA TOLD THE TRUTH

FERNE SALES & MANUFACTURING COMPANY P.O. BOX 113 T.C.B. WEST ORANGE, NJ 07052

'Beam me up, Scotty.' Even though we live in a quiet New England town, I thought someone might try to tear it off. To me, it was certainly worth the risk of making my feelings known, which is basically what a bumper sticker does.

"I still have people pull up next to me and give me the thumbs-up signal. They are usually women. Men pull up and give me the finger. I think I've gotten past any fear of the bumper sticker."

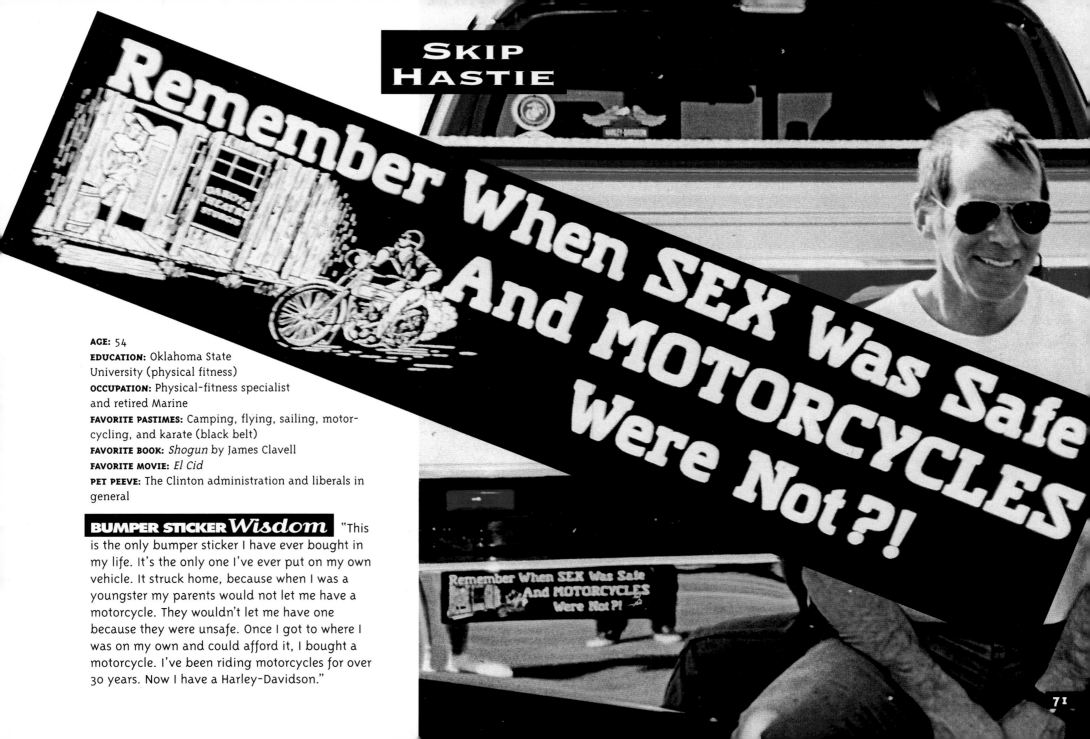

Remember When SEX Was Safe And MOTORCYCLES Were Not?!

AGE: 54

EDUCATION: Oklahoma State University (physical fitness)

OCCUPATION: Physical-fitness specialist and retired Marine

FAVORITE PASTIMES: Camping, flying, sailing, motorcycling, and karate (black belt)

FAVORITE BOOK: *Shogun* by James Clavell

FAVORITE MOVIE: *El Cid*

PET PEEVE: The Clinton administration and liberals in general

BUMPER STICKER *Wisdom* "This is the only bumper sticker I have ever bought in my life. It's the only one I've ever put on my own vehicle. It struck home, because when I was a youngster my parents would not let me have a motorcycle. They wouldn't let me have one because they were unsafe. Once I got to where I was on my own and could afford it, I bought a motorcycle. I've been riding motorcycles for over 30 years. Now I have a Harley-Davidson."

I GAVE UP BOWLING FOR SEX, THE BALLS ARE LIGHTER & I DON'T HAVE TO CHANGE MY SHOES!

I MAY BE SLOW BUT I'M AHEAD OF YOU

JOHNNY RUPE

AGE: 76
EDUCATION: Chehalis High School
OCCUPATION: Truck driver
FAVORITE PASTIMES: "Chasing broads"
FAVORITE BOOK: *Treasure Island* by Robert Louis Stevenson
FAVORITE MOVIE: *Emperor of the North*
PET PEEVE: Drivers who cut you off

BUMPER STICKER *Wisdom*   "I thought collecting bumper stickers was a fun type of game. I get a hoot out of people enjoying them, and I enjoy them myself. I had one on my motor home that said 'I'm a taxidermist, and I'll mount anything.' This guy came up to me in a parking lot and asked if I could mount a duck he shot. I told him that I'm not really a taxidermist and that it was a joke. I had a hell of a time trying to convince him. His wife finally started laughing and figured out what it was."

I'D LOVE TO GAZE INTO YOUR IRISES, KISS YOUR TULIPS, GET INTO YOUR PLANTS AND FONDLE YOUR PETUNIAS

"I NEVER GET LOST" Everybody Tells Me Where To Go.

BEEP!! BEEP!!! YOUR ASS!!

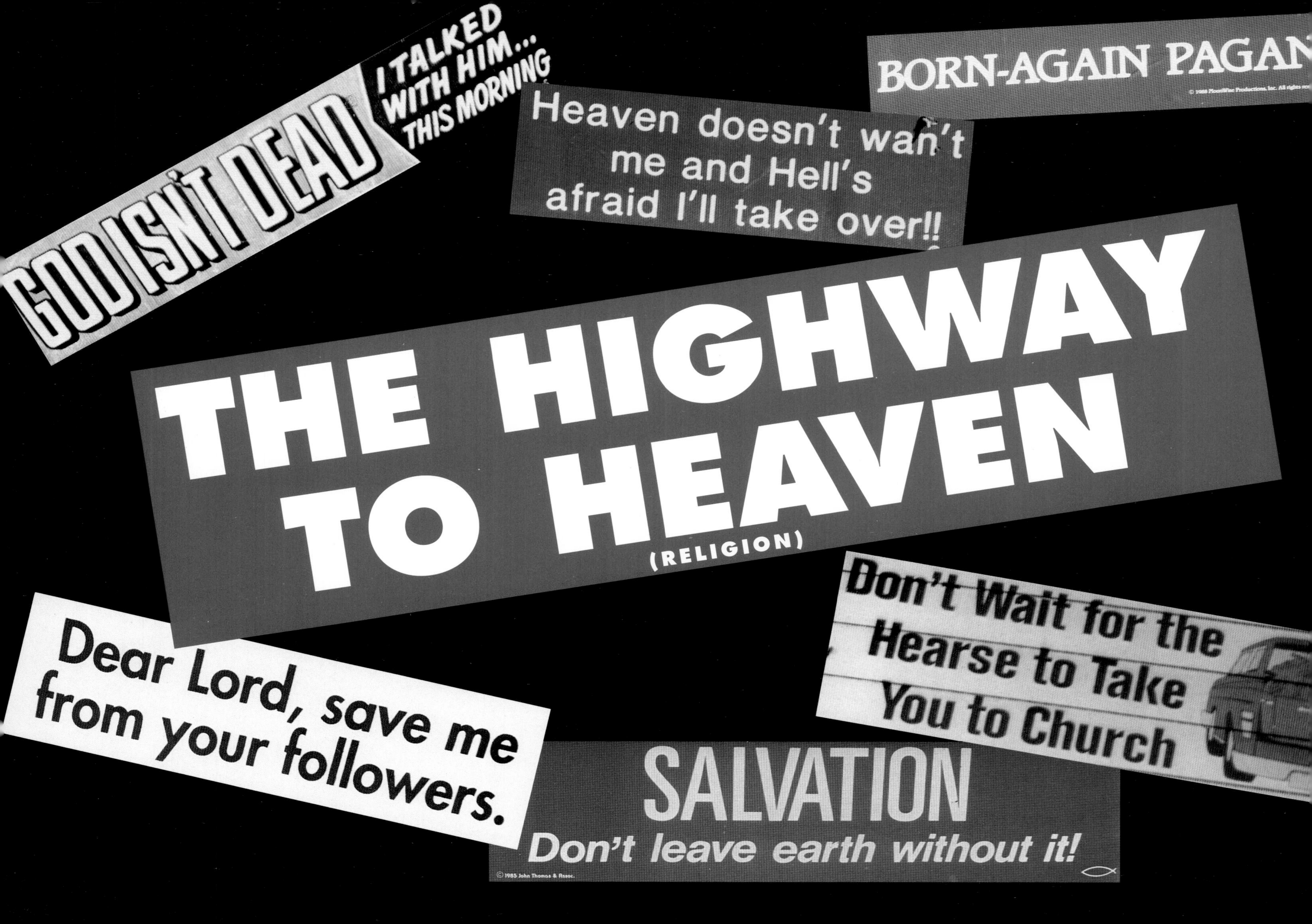

I TALKED WITH HIM... THIS MORNING

GOD ISN'T DEAD

BORN-AGAIN PAGAN

Heaven doesn't wan't me and Hell's afraid I'll take over!!

THE HIGHWAY TO HEAVEN

(RELIGION)

Don't Wait for the Hearse to Take You to Church

Dear Lord, save me from your followers.

SALVATION
Don't leave earth without it!

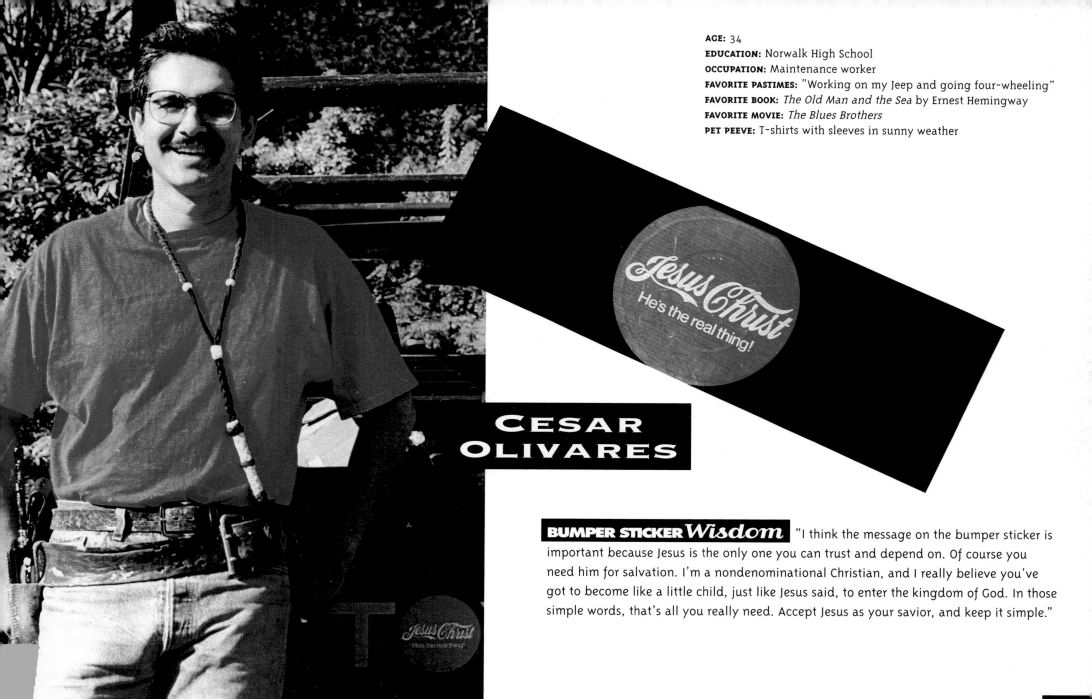

AGE: 34
EDUCATION: Norwalk High School
OCCUPATION: Maintenance worker
FAVORITE PASTIMES: "Working on my Jeep and going four-wheeling"
FAVORITE BOOK: *The Old Man and the Sea* by Ernest Hemingway
FAVORITE MOVIE: *The Blues Brothers*
PET PEEVE: T-shirts with sleeves in sunny weather

CESAR OLIVARES

BUMPER STICKER *Wisdom* "I think the message on the bumper sticker is important because Jesus is the only one you can trust and depend on. Of course you need him for salvation. I'm a nondenominational Christian, and I really believe you've got to become like a little child, just like Jesus said, to enter the kingdom of God. In those simple words, that's all you really need. Accept Jesus as your savior, and keep it simple."

STEVE GARDNER

AGE: 33
EDUCATION: Brigham Young University (journalism)
OCCUPATION: Editor
FAVORITE PASTIMES: Major-league baseball, writing of all kinds, reading, the coast, road trips, Springsteen music, and "The Simpsons"
FAVORITE BOOK: *The Unbearable Lightness of Being* by Milan Kundera
FAVORITE MOVIE: *Field of Dreams*
PET PEEVES: Rigid thinking, political correctness, and baseball strikes

BUMPER STICKER *Wisdom* "I don't think I had ever put a bumper sticker on any of my cars until this one. I put this one on my truck because a couple of my non-Mormon friends dared me to have it on for two weeks. I'm not into polygamy, but I do want to find my soul mate and get married. If nothing else, this is a funny statement about society. I've seen personal ads soliciting things at least as strange as this.

"When I first put it on I was worried that some people might think I was serious, but almost everyone gets that it's a joke. Most of my Mormon friends laugh at it. Some of the women have been uneasy. One guy was pretty upset, because he believes I'm blaspheming something sacred. I've definitely had more conversations about polygamy in the last three weeks than I'd ever had in my life before this. This sticker is a joke. I don't really want more

SINGLE MORMON SEEKS SEVERAL SPOUSES

SINGLE MORMON SEEKS SEVERAL SPOUSES

than one wife. Besides, it's one of the quickest ways to get excommunicated from the Mormon Church. It's been about four weeks since I put the sticker on, and it's probably time to remove it if I ever want to date again."

AGE: 26
EDUCATION: Brown University (international relations)
OCCUPATION: Firefighter and student at San Francisco State University (women's studies)
FAVORITE PASTIMES: Hiking, backpacking, dancing, eating brunch on the weekends, and hanging out with friends
FAVORITE BOOK: *Animal Dreams* by Barbara Kingsolver and *Diet for a New America* by John Robbins
FAVORITE MOVIE: *Adam's Rib* and *It's a Wonderful Life*
PET PEEVE: Empty ice trays and not recycling

KAREN KERR

BUMPER STICKER *Wisdom* "Basically, to me, my bumper sticker reflects the silencing and exclusion of women in our religion and in our society. Patriarchal God religions seem like they wipe out any notion that women could have a positive role in life. In societies where they worshiped goddesses, they've found women's roles were much more valued. I think it's time we looked at other examples in history and other cultures, and looked at more liberating ways of living and practicing spirituality.

My Goddess Gave Birth To Your God!

"I feel we need to do things differently. Women are just as important to our world as men. I don't think our culture recognizes that.

"The bumper sticker is about women's power and brains and strength. The story of women needs to be recognized. The whole idea is, there are goddesses and there are gods. That's why I liked the bumper sticker. It just says it. We wouldn't have much of a population if women weren't giving birth."

BUMPER STICKER *Wisdom* "My sister, Sara, and I bought the bumper sticker at Christian Supply. It means a lot to me because I think it is important to have prayer in school. I think that without God in America our society has taken a steady decline. Prayer should be allowed in school for the students who want it. The bumper sticker shows that there is prayer happening anyway."

As long as there are tests, there will be prayer in schools!

AGE: 15 (Eryn) / 13 (Sara)

EDUCATION: Franklin High School / Kellogg Middle School

OCCUPATION: Students

FAVORITE PASTIMES: Singing, rally, saxophone, running, and acting / Skiing, soccer, singing competitions, and drama

FAVORITE BOOK: *QB Seven* by Leon Uris / *The Jesse Owens Story* by Jesse Owens and Paul G. Neimark

FAVORITE MOVIE: *The Princess Bride* / *Last of the Mohicans*

PET PEEVE: "People who are hypocritical about their pet peeves" / "People who criticize me"

ERYN & SARA WEAVER

As long as there are tests, there will be prayer in schools!

ANNA LENT

AGE: 24
EDUCATION: Portland State University (sociology)
OCCUPATION: Retail sales in natural-fiber clothing
FAVORITE PASTIMES: Photography and beadwork
FAVORITE BOOK: *Temple of My Familiar* by Alice Walker
FAVORITE MOVIE: *Harold and Maude*
PET PEEVE: People who don't use their turn signals

BUMPER STICKER *Wisdom* "Well, I'm a recovering Catholic. So when I saw 'God is coming and is she pissed,' I just had to buy it because it defies the whole notion that God is a man. I've always had this feeling that if there is a God, God is not necessarily a man.

"It also brings up the point that if God is a woman and there is some kind of 'Judgment Day,' she is going to be pretty pissed, because everybody keeps thinking that she is a man. It flirts with the idea that things are not always what you think they are.

"I've gotten a lot of good reactions to the bumper sticker. Mostly it's middle-aged white men, which I found interesting. They enjoy that it makes them think—whether they agree with it or not."

GOD IS COMING AND IS SHE PISSED

THE REVEREND
C. E. LINVILLE

Jesus Loves You, but everyone else thinks you're an asshole.

AGE: 43
EDUCATION: Rio Hondo College (broadcasting)
OCCUPATION: Letter carrier and Universal Life Church minister for Our Lady of Eternal Combustion Church
FAVORITE PASTIMES: Collecting strange and interesting records and being active in the Cacophony Society and the Beater Club
FAVORITE BOOK: *The Gospel Hour* by T. R. Pearson
FAVORITE MOVIE: *Wise Blood*
PET PEEVE: Right-wing Christians

BUMPER STICKER *Wisdom* "I was interested in becoming a minister after being assaulted by a lot of the hardcore religious types I work with. If Jesus came back he'd probably sue most of these people for slander.

"To become a minister through the Universal Life Church all you have to do is sign your name legibly. Also, I registered with the county for five bucks, and so now I can marry people. A justice of the peace charges $75, so I figured I'd just charge $50 and give a full-service wedding. I wear a dinner jacket that is decorated kinda like my car. I give 'em a pretty painless two-minute ceremony. I've married 12 couples.

"The thing I like better is doing short-term marriages. I've got these fancy Our Lady of Eternal Combustion short-term marriage certificates. They are $5 a pop. I've done at least 200 temporary marriages.

"Right-wing Christians were really part of my inspiration for the 'Beware of God' sign in my car's window. One time this old guy came up and said, 'Huh! "Beware of God"—I got me a "Beware of dog" sign and, well, I guess either one of them can sneak up and bite you on the ankles when you're not lookin'.' That sums it up pretty well. There's nothing wrong with believing in God and Christian principles, but when people twist the principles around, you have to watch out."

MARGARETE SCRIVNER

AGE: 67
EDUCATION: Burlington Edison High School
OCCUPATION: Housewife and retired bus driver
FAVORITE PASTIMES: Bowling, fishing, and camping
FAVORITE BOOK: The Bible
FAVORITE MOVIE: *Sister Act 2: Back in the Habit*
PET PEEVE: Swearing

BUMPER STICKER *Wisdom*   "I got the sticker at a family reunion in
Bethany, Missouri, this summer. It gets the message across to people that God's last
name is not Dammit. You know, a lot of people use God's name in vain."

GOD'S LAST NAME IS NOT DAMMIT!

Compliments of CLOCK BAIT SHOP-7910 N. OAK

I'm Glad Mary & Joseph
Were not Pro-Choice

TESTIMONY TIME P.O. BOX 505. ST.ANN. MO. USA 63074

Get Your Rosary
Off My Ovary

THE DIVIDING
LINE
(PRO-CHOICE/PRO-LIFE)

HOICE BEFORE SEX
LIFE AFTER

AGAINST ABORTION?
HAVE A VASECTOMY

MOLLEE KLEIN

AGE: 21
EDUCATION: Cabrillo College (dance and education)
OCCUPATION: Student
FAVORITE PASTIMES: Dance
FAVORITE BOOK: *Handmaid's Tale* by Margaret Atwood
FAVORITE MOVIE: *8 1/2* and other Fellini films
PET PEEVE: Closed-minded people

U.S. OUT OF MY UTERUS

DONNELLY/COLT CUSTOMPRINTING, BOX 188 HAMPTON, CT 06247 203-455-9621

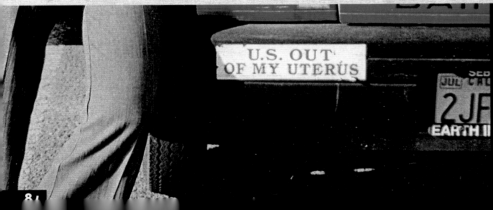

BUMPER STICKER *Wisdom* "I got the bumper sticker because I was raised believing that people have the right to make their own decisions. My mom is a strong feminist and so I have strong feminist beliefs.

"I liked this bumper sticker as opposed to other pro-choice bumper stickers because I thought it related more to making it a nonpolitical issue by saying that abortion is really a woman's choice and not something that should be a public forum. Also, as opposed to other pro-choice bumper stickers, I hope it makes people think about taking something that is such a private issue and putting it on such a public forum. I hope it at least makes people think about the issue even if they don't agree with the sentiment."

ANGEL PETERSON

AGE: 18
EDUCATION: Scappoose High School
OCCUPATION: Student
FAVORITE PASTIMES: Studying the Bible and praying
FAVORITE BOOK: The Bible
FAVORITE MOVIE: *Anne of Green Gables*
PET PEEVE: "Abortion—when a woman takes the life of a child in her hands and acts as though she has the final say as to whether that child lives"

BUMPER STICKER *Wisdom* "The world has gotten so far away from God that we're now worshiping the creations, not the creator. We are acting as though animals are more important than children. People, like the Greenpeace people, are going crazy trying to save the whales, and then they'll slaughter their children so they can continue their education or whatever.

"I can't believe that man has turned his back on God and totally denied the sanctity of what God has ordained. That's not right."

Author's Note: Angel used to have another bumper sticker that said "Salvation: Don't leave Earth without it."

BE A HERO SAVE A WHALE
SAVE A BABY GO TO JAIL

BE A HERO SAVE A WHALE
SAVE A BABY GO TO JAIL

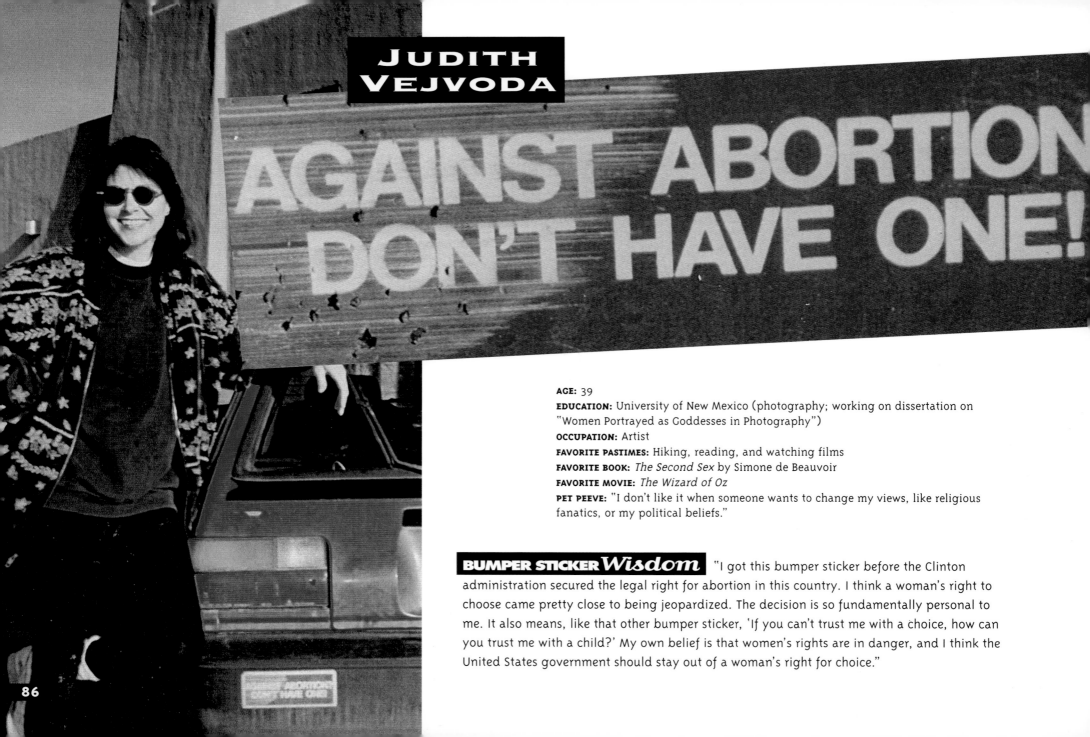

JUDITH VEJVODA

AGAINST ABORTION DON'T HAVE ONE!

AGE: 39
EDUCATION: University of New Mexico (photography; working on dissertation on "Women Portrayed as Goddesses in Photography")
OCCUPATION: Artist
FAVORITE PASTIMES: Hiking, reading, and watching films
FAVORITE BOOK: *The Second Sex* by Simone de Beauvoir
FAVORITE MOVIE: *The Wizard of Oz*
PET PEEVE: "I don't like it when someone wants to change my views, like religious fanatics, or my political beliefs."

BUMPER STICKER *Wisdom* "I got this bumper sticker before the Clinton administration secured the legal right for abortion in this country. I think a woman's right to choose came pretty close to being jeopardized. The decision is so fundamentally personal to me. It also means, like that other bumper sticker, 'If you can't trust me with a choice, how can you trust me with a child?' My own belief is that women's rights are in danger, and I think the United States government should stay out of a woman's right for choice."

SAM McPHERSON

AGE: 41
EDUCATION: Amarillo College (photography)
OCCUPATION: Church custodian
FAVORITE PASTIMES: Woodworking
FAVORITE BOOK: The Bible
FAVORITE MOVIE: *Gone with the Wind*
PET PEEVE: People who claim to be Christian and don't act like it

BUMPER STICKER *Wisdom* "I picked this bumper sticker up at a pro-life booth at the Tri-State Fair. It states what I believe about abortion. I believe that anyone who is supporting pro-choice or abortion and claiming to be a Christian—it doesn't coincide. If you're a Christian, you're against murder. And abortion, in my opinion, is murder. You talk about save the whales, save the seals and everything—well, what are we doing to our own kids? We're killing them."

Pro-Choice OR Christian
-You CAN'T be BOTH

Pro-Choice OR Christian
-You CAN'T be BOTH

ANDRIANA KRUGER

BUMPER STICKER *Wisdom* "It's just a freedom of choice to be responsible enough that I can make an educated choice of my own instead of having to have a law that says 'No, you can't have an abortion.' The right to choice is interesting. There are these men on television, large middle-aged men, and they are fanatical, foaming at the mouth about abortion. It's like, how do you know? Are you the 16-year-old girl who was raped or molested by a relative? You don't know. There are so many different things that happen. A life is precious, but if it's not a welcome life, what good is it?"

AGE: 33
EDUCATION: Endicott College (photography and psychology)
OCCUPATION: Production manager at an advertising studio and mom-to-be
FAVORITE PASTIMES: Hiking and skiing
FAVORITE BOOK: *Like Water for Chocolate* by Laura Esquivel
PET PEEVE: Narrow-mindedness

If you can't trust me with a choice, how can you trust me with a child?

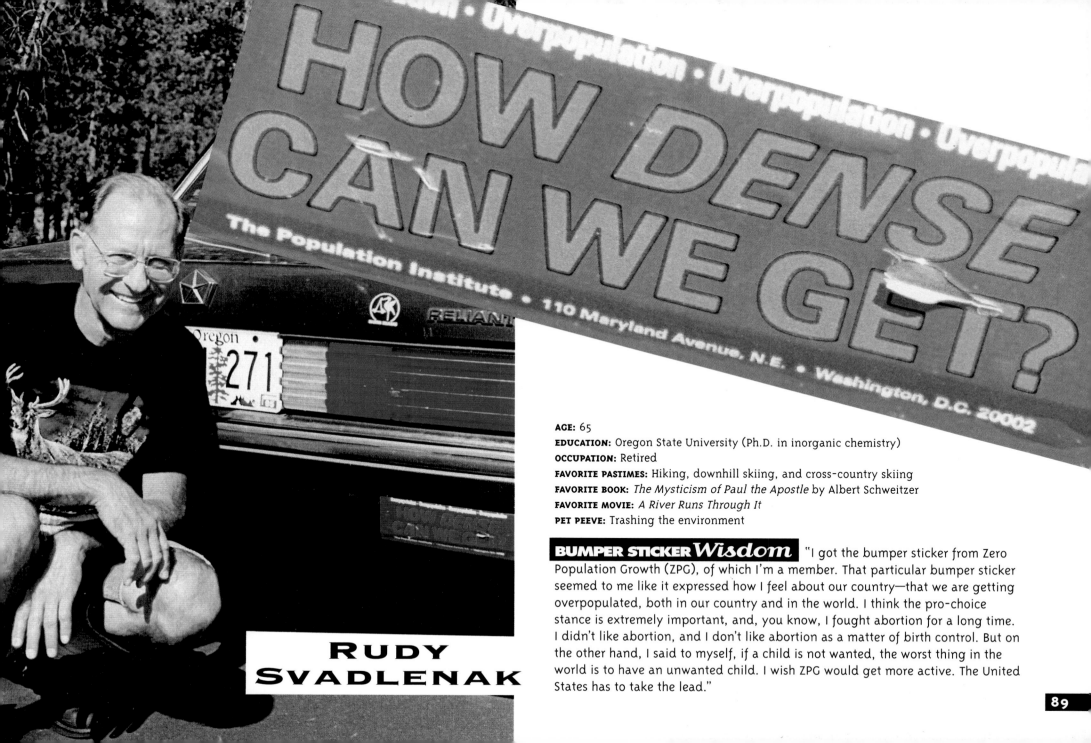

HOW DENSE CAN WE GET?

Overpopulation · Overpopulation · Overpopulation · Overpopulation

The Population Institute · 110 Maryland Avenue, N.E. · Washington, D.C. 20002

AGE: 65
EDUCATION: Oregon State University (Ph.D. in inorganic chemistry)
OCCUPATION: Retired
FAVORITE PASTIMES: Hiking, downhill skiing, and cross-country skiing
FAVORITE BOOK: *The Mysticism of Paul the Apostle* by Albert Schweitzer
FAVORITE MOVIE: *A River Runs Through It*
PET PEEVE: Trashing the environment

BUMPER STICKER *Wisdom* "I got the bumper sticker from Zero Population Growth (ZPG), of which I'm a member. That particular bumper sticker seemed to me like it expressed how I feel about our country—that we are getting overpopulated, both in our country and in the world. I think the pro-choice stance is extremely important, and, you know, I fought abortion for a long time. I didn't like abortion, and I don't like abortion as a matter of birth control. But on the other hand, I said to myself, if a child is not wanted, the worst thing in the world is to have an unwanted child. I wish ZPG would get more active. The United States has to take the lead."

RUDY SVADLENAK

KATE BREIMAYER

AGE: 24
EDUCATION: Pacific Northwest College of Art
OCCUPATION: Picture framer
FAVORITE PASTIMES: Playing bass guitar and going to clarinet concerts
FAVORITE BOOK: Books by Dorothy Parker
FAVORITE MOVIE: *Delicatessen*
PET PEEVE: "I ♥ whales" stickers and any other "I ♥_____" stickers

SAVE THE PLANET KILL YOURSELF

SAVE THE PLANET
KILL YOURSELF

Author's Note: Kate tells me that her friend Chris Korda wrote and produced this bumper sticker. She says he is a transvestite and a musician who has produced a CD called "Demons in My Head."

BUMPER STICKER *Wisdom* "Mostly I liked this bumper sticker because most of the problems people complain about on their bumper stickers are just overpopulation. The environment, save this, save that—we can all take up one cause and go for it all the way and preach it to everyone, but basically there is just not enough food, water, and land. I think the Chinese are right. We are stupid!"

ONLY ELEPHANTS SHOULD WEAR IVORY

AFRICAN WILDLIFE FOUNDATION

If trees are a renewable resource, where have all the forests gone?

© PHRESH STICKERS 1-800-600-7962

SCENIC ROUTE

(ENVIRONMENT)

ON'T CUSS THE FARMER WITH YOUR MOUTH FULL

MEAT IS MURDER

AGE: 48
EDUCATION: University of Oregon (Ph.D. in biology) and Oregon State University (postdoctorate in biochemistry)
OCCUPATION: Marine mammal specialist at the Hatfield Marine Science Center and professor of fisheries and wildlife at Oregon State University
FAVORITE PASTIMES: Restoring sports cars, photography, and cross-country skiing
FAVORITE BOOK: *Endurance: Shackleton's Incredible Voyage* by Alfred Lansing
FAVORITE MOVIE: *2001: A Space Odyssey* and *Schindler's List*
PET PEEVE: "Painfully slow traffic pretty well drives me nuts."

BRUCE MATE

SAVE THE WHALES

Author's Note: Bruce Mate was the first person to use satellites to track whales. His work has been featured in National Geographic, Smithsonian, and Oceanus. He was also the focus of an award-winning Nova special on PBS.

BUMPER STICKER *Wisdom* "I think the whales are one of the symbols of the environmental movement. As a marine biologist my career is built around trying to identify critical habitats and making sure that we don't lose the animals through benign neglect. 'Save the whales' makes it sound like 'Don't hunt them,' but not hunting them isn't adequate to ensure their protection. So if they are going to exist in the future, we have to also provide places for them to live. My goal is to see that that is done in such a way that human development takes them into consideration. I don't limit it to whales, but whales are probably the most visible rallying point for people and a symbol that they can strongly identify with. I take 'Save the whales' very personally even though it is also my profession."

BUMPER STICKER *Wisdom* "We're very worried in our society about taking care of the planet and taking care of the animals and the whales and everything—but we're not that worried about taking care of human beings. I think it has put us into jeopardy, and if we don't have decent human beings, responsible human beings, human beings who care about other people, it's not going to do us much good to have a planet on which to live or whales to watch. I think we have lost our ability to take responsibility."

SAVE THE HUMANS

Peace Resource Project P.O. Box 1122 Arcata, CA 95521 USA

AGE: 57
EDUCATION: University of California at Riverside (working on a certificate in gerontology)
OCCUPATION: Nurse/director at Eisenhower Five Star Clinic (an adult day-care center for persons with Alzheimer's and Parkinson's diseases)
FAVORITE PASTIMES: Reading and walking
FAVORITE BOOK: *Wait Until Morning* by Beryl Markham
FAVORITE MOVIE: *Casablanca*
PET PEEVE: People who are intolerant of the aging community

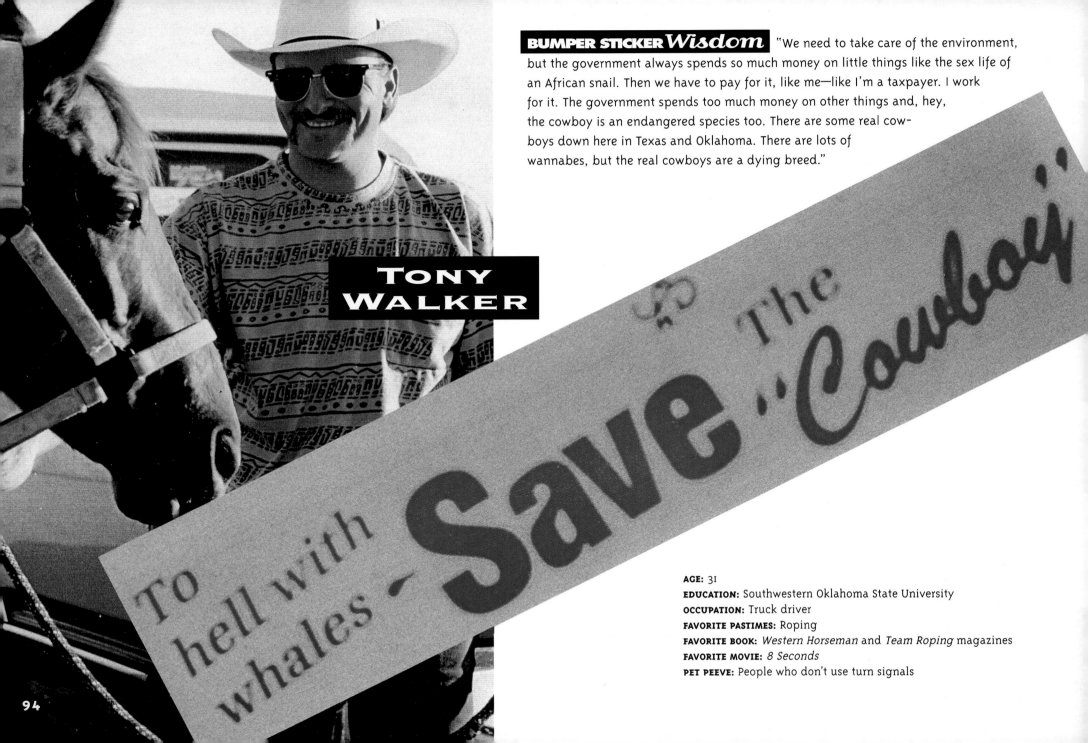

BUMPER STICKER *Wisdom* "We need to take care of the environment, but the government always spends so much money on little things like the sex life of an African snail. Then we have to pay for it, like me—like I'm a taxpayer. I work for it. The government spends too much money on other things and, hey, the cowboy is an endangered species too. There are some real cowboys down here in Texas and Oklahoma. There are lots of wannabes, but the real cowboys are a dying breed."

TONY WALKER

To hell with whales - Save "Cowboy"

AGE: 31
EDUCATION: Southwestern Oklahoma State University
OCCUPATION: Truck driver
FAVORITE PASTIMES: Roping
FAVORITE BOOK: *Western Horseman* and *Team Roping* magazines
FAVORITE MOVIE: *8 Seconds*
PET PEEVE: People who don't use turn signals

BUMPER STICKER *Wisdom* "It just tells everybody that I'm a cowboy."

RODNEY SCRUGGS

AGE: 32
EDUCATION: Liberal High School
OCCUPATION: Farm hand and welder
FAVORITE PASTIMES: Snowmobiling and horse riding
FAVORITE BOOK: Books by Louis L'Amour
FAVORITE MOVIE: *8 Seconds*
PET PEEVE: None

YOU'RE DAMN RIGHT I'M A COWBOY

Author's Note: Rodney has a second bumper sticker that says "Don't cuss the farmer with your mouth full."

YOU'RE DAMN RIGHT I'M A COWBOY

"I guess it's more just trying to get people to support the beef industry. It's kind of promoting the industry. A little humor there. I think people are more health-conscious, and they get the wrong ideas about beef being bad for you. I really don't think it's like that. Most people out here in Oklahoma are pretty supportive of beef."

(Support beef—run over a chicken)

LUKE CAMPBELL

AGE: 27
EDUCATION: Sun City Baptist Church School
OCCUPATION: Cowboy
FAVORITE PASTIMES: Breaking horses, hunting, and fishing
FAVORITE BOOK: Books by Louis L'Amour
FAVORITE MOVIE: *The Cowboys*
PET PEEVE: "I'd like people to just be able to be themselves."

SUPPORT BEEF
RUN OVER A CHICKEN.

Author's Note: *It was a Saturday morning in Beaver, Oklahoma, and I was seated in a booth at the Beaver Barbecue Pit, drinking a cup of coffee and staring at a plate of hash browns and gravy, when in walked five cowboys—straight out of Lonesome Dove. Now, I'm not a terribly religious person, but I said to myself, "Dear God, please let them have a bumper sticker." Their yellow Ford pickup was parked outside, and as I rounded the back bumper I saw the remains of an old, shredded sticker that read "Support beef—run over a chicken." Well, I ran back into the restaurant and convinced Luke Campbell, the owner of the truck, to let me photograph and interview him. He agreed, much to the bemusement of his friends. Luke, who is polite to the point of "Yes ma'am" and "No ma'am," and I proceeded with the interview. By the time we had finished, the other cowboys had joined us at the back of the truck. One of them, a bashful fellow in tall green boots, "moseyed" over and said, "Excuse me, ma'am, but we have a bumper sticker, and we'd like to be in your book, too." Then he grinned and said, "Our bumper sticker says 'Support America—run over Clinton.'"*

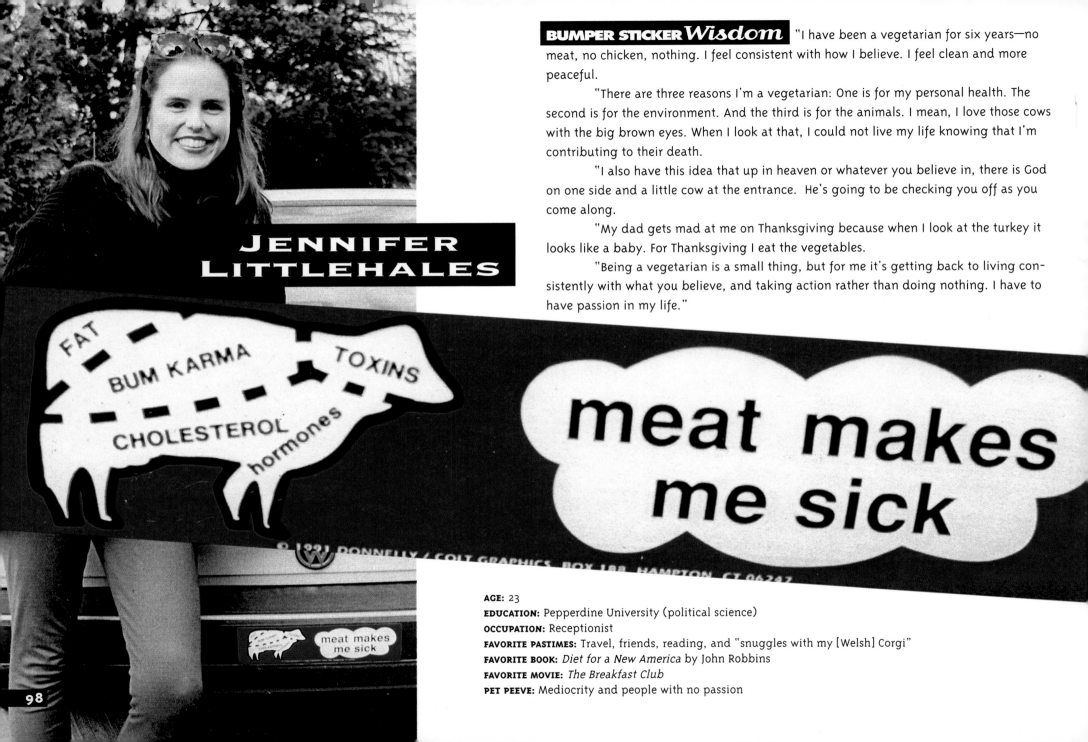

JENNIFER LITTLEHALES

BUMPER STICKER *Wisdom* "I have been a vegetarian for six years—no meat, no chicken, nothing. I feel consistent with how I believe. I feel clean and more peaceful.

"There are three reasons I'm a vegetarian: One is for my personal health. The second is for the environment. And the third is for the animals. I mean, I love those cows with the big brown eyes. When I look at that, I could not live my life knowing that I'm contributing to their death.

"I also have this idea that up in heaven or whatever you believe in, there is God on one side and a little cow at the entrance. He's going to be checking you off as you come along.

"My dad gets mad at me on Thanksgiving because when I look at the turkey it looks like a baby. For Thanksgiving I eat the vegetables.

"Being a vegetarian is a small thing, but for me it's getting back to living consistently with what you believe, and taking action rather than doing nothing. I have to have passion in my life."

FAT
BUM KARMA
TOXINS
CHOLESTEROL
hormones

meat makes me sick

© 1991 DONNELLY / COLT GRAPHICS, BOX 188, HAMPTON, CT 06247

meat makes me sick

AGE: 23
EDUCATION: Pepperdine University (political science)
OCCUPATION: Receptionist
FAVORITE PASTIMES: Travel, friends, reading, and "snuggles with my [Welsh] Corgi"
FAVORITE BOOK: *Diet for a New America* by John Robbins
FAVORITE MOVIE: *The Breakfast Club*
PET PEEVE: Mediocrity and people with no passion

BUMPER STICKER *Wisdom* "Well, when I seen it, I thought that every-body deserves a steak. But if these environmentalists keep it up, there isn't going to be any steak for anybody."

"YOU DESERVE A STEAK TODAY!"

AMPBELL TRANSPORTATION

WEISER LIVESTOCK COMMISSION

AGE: 40
EDUCATION: Nampa High School
OCCUPATION: Rancher
FAVORITE PASTIMES: "Roping with my boy"
FAVORITE BOOK: *Owyhee Trails: The West's Forgotten Corner* by Mike Hanley and Ellis Lucia
FAVORITE MOVIE: *The Man from Snowy River*
PET PEEVE: Environmentalists

Author's Note: *I met Pat driving down the freeway in Idaho, along with his 14-year-old son and his dog. He was the quintessential cowboy, as considerate as could be and straight-forward in his answers. He didn't hesitate once in his response to my questions.*

"YOU DESERVE A STEAK TODAY!"

AGE: 35
EDUCATION: Galt High School
OCCUPATION: Rancher
FAVORITE PASTIMES: Riding, roping, and breeding horses
FAVORITE BOOK: *Galloway* by Louis L'Amour
FAVORITE MOVIE: *Lonesome Dove*
PET PEEVE: People who make mountains out of molehills

MANUEL AZEVEDO

Hungry & Out of Work? Eat An Environmentalist

BUMPER STICKER *Wisdom* "This bumper sticker tells a story because the environmentalists don't have a clue what goes on out here. They have big money and they have nothing better to do than sit at their computers in a city and yap about something they know nothing about.

"We run cattle up in the Sierras. There are places in the mountains they've shut down to grazing that are so 'brushy,' the deer won't travel there anymore. It's nothing but a fire hazard.

"The environmentalists want to walk up the trail, but they don't want to get any crap on their feet. Why the hell don't they stay in town?

"A lot of ranchers have had to sell out because of the environmentalists. You shut a ranch down and you're shutting off the gas guy, the insurance man, the ranch hands, the tire guy. The environmentalists don't realize how many people a rancher takes care of and how many people he feeds.

"We take care of the country like it's ours because that's our livelihood. All we're trying to do is make an honest living."

BUMPER STICKER *Wisdom*

"It's not like cows get down in the river and eat salmon. It's the impact the cows have on the fishes' habitat. If you have this vision in your mind of what a good trout-producing or salmon-producing stream looks like: It's got deep pools; it's got cool, clean water; it's got good bank structure with a lot of root structures on the vegetation around it.

"When cows come in and abuse a situation, which happens throughout the arid West, they first take all the grasses out. Then they take out the browse, which are the young trees, the alders, and the willows. Then the old trees die and fall over. There is nothing to replace them, and pretty soon you've just got bare dirt banks. When the high water comes in the spring, the banks erode. The silt gets into the spawning gravels and chokes out the eggs. In the summertime there is no canopy over the stream so the water temperatures are elevated.

"You get a lot of pollution from the fecal chloroform and the other pollutants caused directly by the animals. The list goes on and on, but basically the cows trash out the streams."

CRAIG LACY

COWS KILL SALMON

©1993 OREGON NATURAL DESERT ORGANIZATION/5% LEFT

NBC 138 OREGON

COWS KILL SALMON

AGE: 48

EDUCATION: San Francisco State University (business) and Oregon State University (fisheries)

OCCUPATION: Fly-fishing outfitter, student, and father

FAVORITE PASTIMES: Fly fishing, enjoying nature, photography, bird watching, and bowhunting

FAVORITE BOOK: *The Monkey Wrench Gang* by Edward Abbey

FAVORITE MOVIE: *A River Runs Through It*

PET PEEVE: "The way we treat public lands and the abuses on national forests and BLM land"

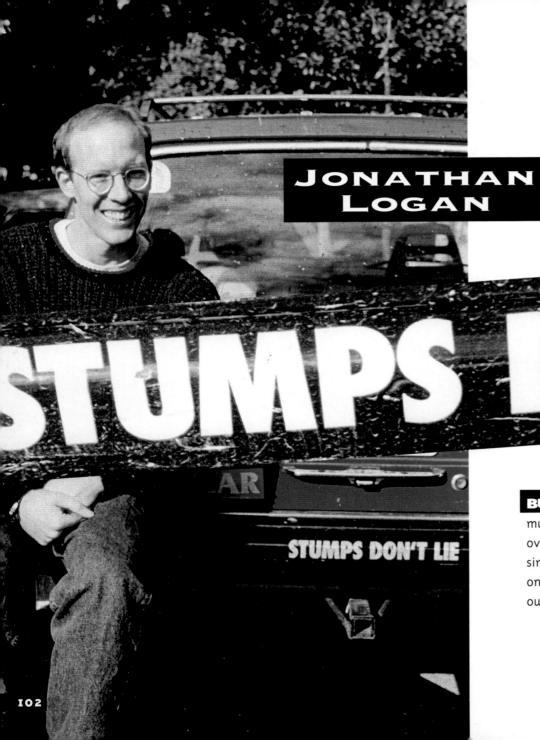

JONATHAN LOGAN

AGE: 32
EDUCATION: Lewis and Clark College Northwestern School of Law
OCCUPATION: Attorney and student
FAVORITE PASTIMES: Growing exotic garlics, studying philosophy, having fun, and causing fun
FAVORITE BOOK: *Ishmael* by Daniel Quinn and *Limits to Growth* compiled by the Club of Rome
FAVORITE MOVIE: *Mindwalk*
PET PEEVE: Short-term thinking, e.g., nuclear power and manufactured homes

BUMPER STICKER *Wisdom* "Who knows what's true anymore? There is so much information and too much data about the environmental problem. It is a complete overload. People want something simple. The bumper sticker, 'Stumps don't lie,' is very simple. It just means one thing: Look, look. Forget all the words; just perceive what's going on. When you see what's going on you can understand the devastation. We are shredding our culture; we are shredding the environment. It's nuts. We need to keep it simple."

ROBERT HICKERSON

AGE: 45
EDUCATION: Brookings High School
OCCUPATION: Truck driver and heavy-equipment operator
FAVORITE PASTIMES: Hunting and fishing
FAVORITE BOOK: Books by Louis L'Amour
FAVORITE MOVIE: Louis L'Amour movies and war movies
PET PEEVE: Wasted spent money

BUMPER STICKER *Wisdom* "The logging and timber industry is down the drain because the environmentalists got so powerful. They pick anything like the spotted owl or the marlet, and they make such a big case about it. They're so rich and famous now that they don't care about the working people. They're so big you can't go against them. I don't know what the solution is."

I ♥ SPOTTED OWLS FRIED IN EXON OIL!

AGE: 43
EDUCATION: Oregon State University (business administration and criminal law)
OCCUPATION: Transit supervisor for Tri-Met (a public transportation district)
FAVORITE PASTIMES: Chess, live music, camping, and things that are fun
FAVORITE BOOK: *My Bondage and My Freedom* by Frederick Douglass
FAVORITE MOVIE: *The Terminator*
PET PEEVE: Bad drivers

219 Cars Are At Home Because I'm On The Road.

BUMPER STICKER *Wisdom*

"Americans are in love with their cars. You know, guys love their trucks. We at Tri-Met [public transportation] are trying to increase the ridership on our bus system by letting people know through our bumper sticker that 219 cars are off the road because of one bus. We're helping keep the streets clean and clear and the air quality good. We want people to look at the bumper sticker and know that by taking public transportation they help themselves and the environment."

STAN WHEELER

AGE: 36
EDUCATION: State University of New York (psychology)
OCCUPATION: Volunteer at Laughing Horse Books (an alternative bookstore) and activist for women's issues and social change
FAVORITE PASTIMES: Reading and writing
FAVORITE BOOK: *Teenage Liberation Handbook* by Grace Llewellyn
FAVORITE MOVIE: *Malcolm X*
PET PEEVE: Automobiles

DORCAS MALOTT

QUESTION INTERNAL COMBUSTION

BUMPER STICKER *Wisdom* "The bumper sticker is partly about how we do our transportation in this country. But it's also about 'Question the way things are' and try to imagine how they could be different, and different in a positive way. I mean, imagine this bookstore in a community where we would have only foot traffic. We wouldn't have to worry about cars running over us. And then maybe there would be gardens out front and maybe we're composting. Just question the way things are and try to picture a different way to the same thing or a different way to do it altogether."

JAVIER HERNANDEZ

BUMPER STICKER *Wisdom* "I got the bumper sticker from United Farm Workers at a meeting. They gave it free. You know Cesar Chavez. They gave it to people to put it on their bumpers because of the chemicals the big companies put on the grapes. My wife, you know, works in the grapes, and her skin gets rashes. Don't buy grapes, because all the companies that buy grapes don't have contracts with the union."

NO GRAPES

United Farm Workers of America AFL-CIO P.O. Box 62 La Paz Keene C.A. 93531

NO GRAPES

Author's Note: *Javier's other bumper sticker proudly announced "My child is an honor student at _____."*

AGE: 33
EDUCATION: (Eighth grade)
OCCUPATION: Fruit-orchard worker
FAVORITE PASTIMES: Going to dances
FAVORITE BOOK: The Bible
FAVORITE MOVIE: Clint Eastwood movies
PET PEEVE: Loud music

War is the real enemy.

If Guns Are Outlawed Only Outlaws Will Have Guns

ROUGH ROAD AHEAD

(PEACE)

FEED THE PEOPLE NOT THE PENTAGON

Join the Army; travel to exotic, distant lands; meet exciting, unusual people, and kill them.

BACK BY POPULAR DEMAND

Peace Resource Project P.O. Box 1122 Arcata, CA 95521 US

CUSTOMSTICKERS BOX 188, HAMPTON, CT 06247 (203) 455-9621

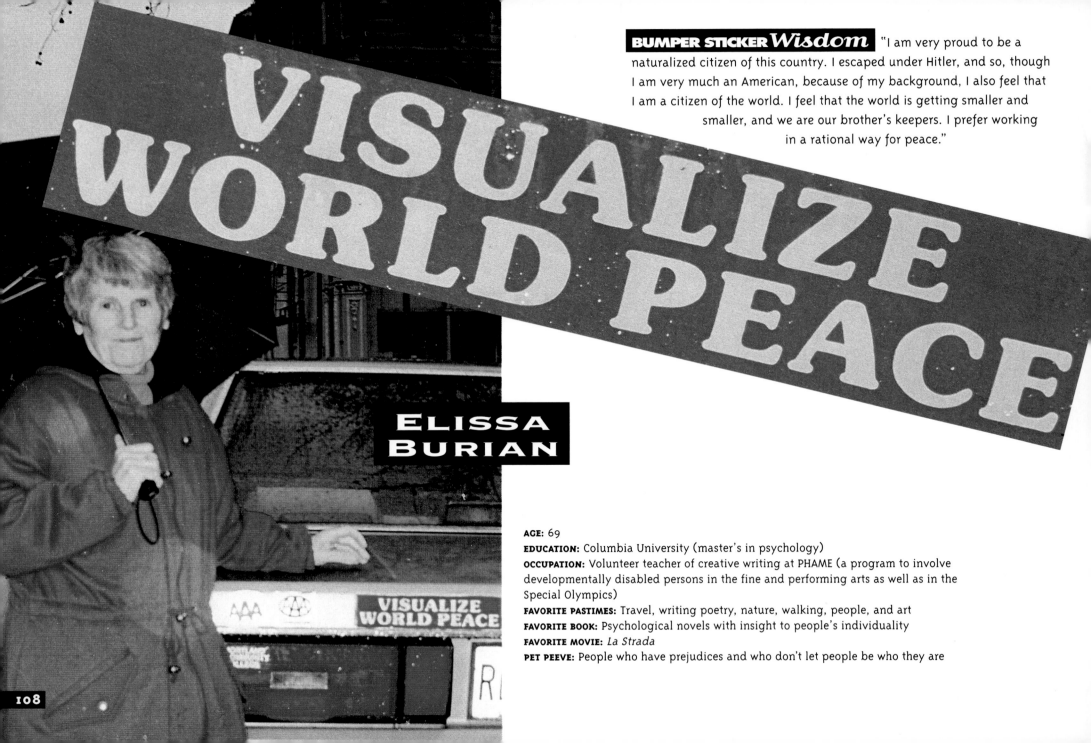

VISUALIZE WORLD PEACE

BUMPER STICKER *Wisdom* "I am very proud to be a naturalized citizen of this country. I escaped under Hitler, and so, though I am very much an American, because of my background, I also feel that I am a citizen of the world. I feel that the world is getting smaller and smaller, and we are our brother's keepers. I prefer working in a rational way for peace."

ELISSA BURIAN

AGE: 69
EDUCATION: Columbia University (master's in psychology)
OCCUPATION: Volunteer teacher of creative writing at PHAME (a program to involve developmentally disabled persons in the fine and performing arts as well as in the Special Olympics)
FAVORITE PASTIMES: Travel, writing poetry, nature, walking, people, and art
FAVORITE BOOK: Psychological novels with insight to people's individuality
FAVORITE MOVIE: *La Strada*
PET PEEVE: People who have prejudices and who don't let people be who they are

AGE: 44
EDUCATION: Oregon Health Sciences University
OCCUPATION: Cardiologist
FAVORITE PASTIMES: Fishing and music
FAVORITE BOOK: *This Boy's Life* by Tobias Wolfe
FAVORITE MOVIE: *The Conformist*
PET PEEVE: Hypocrisy

Author's Note: *Bill told me he has two other favorite bumper stickers: "Honk if you're Jesus" and "Born OK the first time."*

BILL SIMKOFF

VISUALIZE WHIRLED PEAS

REALITY CHECK, Rt. 9, Box 81A, Santa Fe. NM 87505

BUMPER STICKER *Wisdom*

"You've probably seen the identical bumper sticker, which is the same color, same white lettering on blue background, and says 'Visualize world peace,' and I think it is just one of those vacuous, empty, gobbledegook, warm-fuzzy-emotion-type things. Like what does it mean? Visualize world peace? What are you talking about? Speak English, you know? I thought if people could visualize world peace then it would be just as worthwhile to visualize whirled peas. Just this green blur of crap—it had a lot of similarities."

VISUALIZE WHIRLED PEAS

RICK MOORE

AGE: 34
EDUCATION: David Douglas High School
OCCUPATION: Real-estate agent
FAVORITE PASTIMES: Snowboarding
FAVORITE BOOK: Books by Zig Ziglar
PET PEEVE: "I really like people, but I don't like people who are illogical or tunnel-visioned."

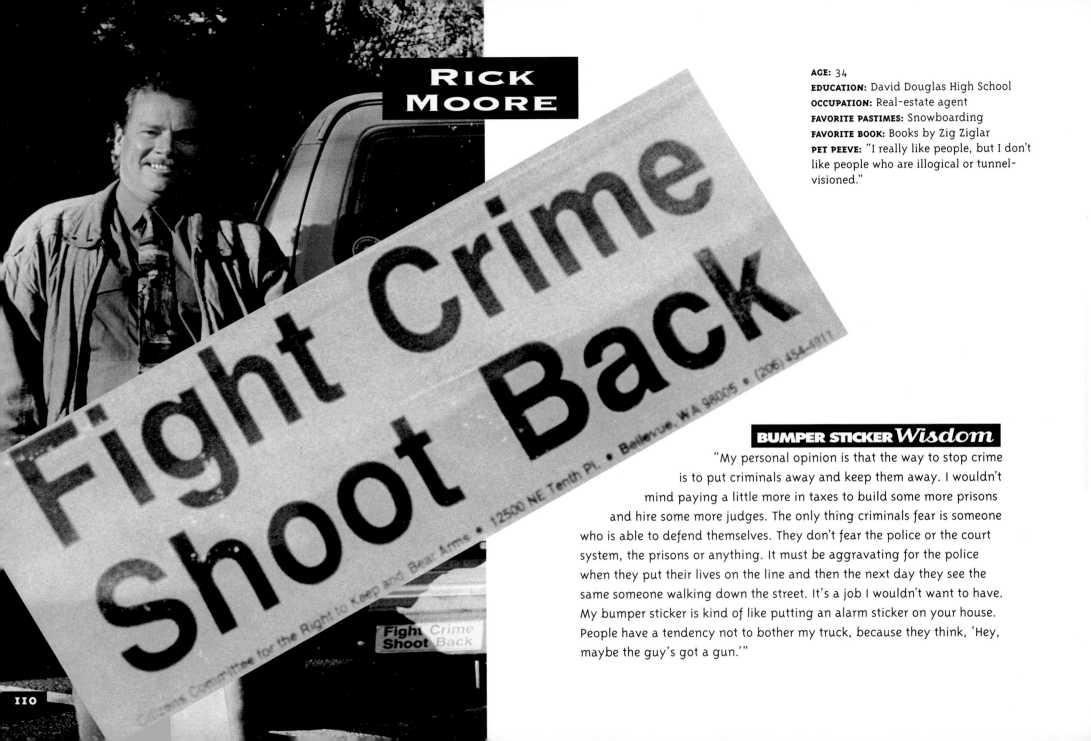

Fight Crime Shoot Back

Citizens Committee for the Right to Keep and Bear Arms • 12500 NE Tenth Pl. • Bellevue, WA 98005 • (206) 454-4911

BUMPER STICKER *Wisdom*

"My personal opinion is that the way to stop crime is to put criminals away and keep them away. I wouldn't mind paying a little more in taxes to build some more prisons and hire some more judges. The only thing criminals fear is someone who is able to defend themselves. They don't fear the police or the court system, the prisons or anything. It must be aggravating for the police when they put their lives on the line and then the next day they see the same someone walking down the street. It's a job I wouldn't want to have. My bumper sticker is kind of like putting an alarm sticker on your house. People have a tendency not to bother my truck, because they think, 'Hey, maybe the guy's got a gun.'"

BUMPER STICKER *Wisdom* "We moved here from Washington, D.C.—the murder capital of the United States. My husband and I both grew up in hunting and fishing families. My dad was a die-hard member, and I say *was*, of the NRA. But this is different. Specifically, now, I'm talking about assault weapons. That's not a sporting weapon. Those are military weapons made for killing as many people as possible. Also handguns—handguns are not for anything but to kill another human being. They're the ones causing most of the problems. I am not a fanatic. I just feel strongly about it. I'm doing it for my kids."

SHARON STEUSSY

Author's Note: *Sharon's husband is a graduate of the U.S. Naval Academy and a career military man.*

Guns. They're killing us.
Join Dehere Gun Fighters of America
Call 1-800-WHY-GUNS

AGE: 43
EDUCATION: University of California at San Diego (international communications)
OCCUPATION: Housewife
FAVORITE PASTIMES: Gardening and birding
FAVORITE BOOK: Books by Tom Clancy
FAVORITE MOVIE: *Planes, Trains & Automobiles*
PET PEEVE: The self-slaughter of people by weapons

Guns. They're killing us.
Join Dehere Gun Fighters of America
Call 1-800-WHY-GUNS

Ted Kennedy's Car Has Killed More People Than MY GUN!

© 1992

Printed in USA

BUMPER STICKER Wisdom "I bought the bumper sticker at a gun show. I bought it because that was when the crime bill was being debated in Congress. I was just trying to make a point that, just like it wasn't Ted Kennedy's car that killed Mary Jo Kopechne on Chappaquiddick, it's not the gun, it's the person behind it.

"Guns don't cause crime any more than flies cause garbage. Also, I don't particularly like Ted Kennedy."

HAROLD ASHFORD

AGE: 44
EDUCATION: Oregon State University (business)
OCCUPATION: Certified public accountant
FAVORITE PASTIMES: Hunting, fishing, and horseback riding
FAVORITE BOOK: *Guns, Crime, and Freedom* by Wayne LaPierre
FAVORITE MOVIE: *The Blues Brothers*
PET PEEVE: People who aren't willing to listen to both sides of issues and people who don't vote

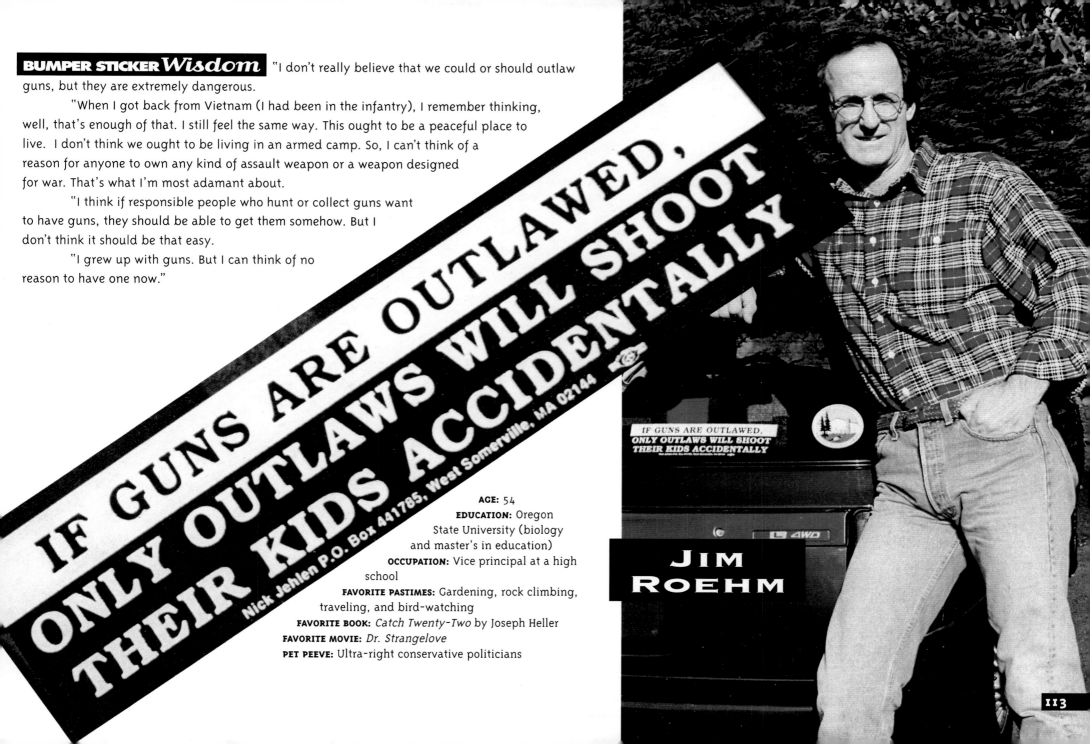

BUMPER STICKER *Wisdom* "I don't really believe that we could or should outlaw guns, but they are extremely dangerous.

"When I got back from Vietnam (I had been in the infantry), I remember thinking, well, that's enough of that. I still feel the same way. This ought to be a peaceful place to live. I don't think we ought to be living in an armed camp. So, I can't think of a reason for anyone to own any kind of assault weapon or a weapon designed for war. That's what I'm most adamant about.

"I think if responsible people who hunt or collect guns want to have guns, they should be able to get them somehow. But I don't think it should be that easy.

"I grew up with guns. But I can think of no reason to have one now."

IF GUNS ARE OUTLAWED, ONLY OUTLAWS WILL SHOOT THEIR KIDS ACCIDENTALLY

Nick Jehlen P.O. Box 441785, West Somerville, MA 02144

AGE: 54
EDUCATION: Oregon State University (biology and master's in education)
OCCUPATION: Vice principal at a high school
FAVORITE PASTIMES: Gardening, rock climbing, traveling, and bird-watching
FAVORITE BOOK: *Catch Twenty-Two* by Joseph Heller
FAVORITE MOVIE: *Dr. Strangelove*
PET PEEVE: Ultra-right conservative politicians

JIM ROEHM

J. GAUT

AGE: 34
EDUCATION: University of Texas (international business)
OCCUPATION: Commercial real-estate agent
FAVORITE PASTIMES: Hunting, sailing, and fishing
FAVORITE BOOK: *Megatrends* by John Naisbitt
FAVORITE MOVIE: *Papillon*
PET PEEVE: Liars

BUMPER STICKER *Wisdom* "A friend of mine, an attorney, started this group to protect landowners' rights. The government keeps taking land away, saying you can't hunt here because the spotted owl is here—that kind of stuff. The main thing, I guess, was landowners' rights. I own some land and I just want to be able to do what I want to do on it. I've taken my oldest son hunting with me. He likes being outside a lot."

SHARE THE HERITAGE
TAKE A KID HUNTING

TEXAS WILDLIFE ASSOCIATION

San Antonio, TX

TOM ALLINGER

AGE: 34
EDUCATION: Loara High School
OCCUPATION: Electrician
FAVORITE PASTIMES: Trains
FAVORITE BOOK: The Bible and books by Stephen King
FAVORITE MOVIE: *Silent Running*
PET PEEVE: People who don't use turn signals

BUMPER STICKER *Wisdom* "I'm a member of the National Rifle Association. I believe in the right to own guns, but I'm not quite as hardheaded about it as some guys are. It's an individual right. Um, I just thought it would be humorous and a play on the words 'A right to bear arms,' so I found the bumper sticker in a store, and I thought it was pretty funny."

Support the Right To Arm Bears

Author's Note: Tom actually looks a bit like the smiling bear on the bumper sticker. He chose to combine humor and his belief in each individual's right to bear arms to make his point.

LOREN HUGHES

AGE: 46
EDUCATION: Eastern Wyoming College (law enforcement)
OCCUPATION: Motorcycle mechanic
FAVORITE PASTIMES: Diving and "playing with my kids"
FAVORITE BOOK: *The Vampire Lestat* by Anne Rice
FAVORITE MOVIE: *Star Wars*
PET PEEVE: Liberals

BUMPER STICKER *Wisdom* "The reason that bumper sticker is on my car is because at one time there was a rash of flag burning here in the South. A number of my relatives fought for the flag and died for it, and I fought in Vietnam. Not being particularly patriotic or anything, it's still a symbol that means a lot to a lot of people. Consequently I'm willing to thump somebody over it."

FLAG BURNERS BEWARE!!!

IF I SEE YOU BURNING THE FLAG OF MY COUNTRY,
I WILL USE MY "FREEDOM OF EXPRESSION"
TO ADJUST YOUR ATTITUDE!!

THIS IS <u>NOT</u> A THREAT...IT'S A PROMISE!!

VETERANS OF THE VIETNAM WAR INC.
• PEOPLE WHO CARE •

JIMMY ALLEN COLLINS

Author's Note: *I saw Jimmy Allen leave his pickup and go into Bob's Cafe in Wallowa, Oregon. There was a rifle in the front seat, "for coyotes." He was proud of the time he served in Vietnam but angry with people who didn't support the men who risked their lives. At a military camp he was involved in an altercation with a flag-burner. In this case, both the words and the graphic shaking fist seemed to express Jimmy Allen's views exactly. His camouflage T-shirt said "Made in America."*

AGE: 45
EDUCATION: Wallowa High School
OCCUPATION: Lumber-mill worker
FAVORITE PASTIMES: Hunting, fishing, and watching sports
FAVORITE MOVIE: *Dances with Wolves*
PET PEEVE: "When I see somebody degrading our flag—I spent 27 months in Vietnam."

BUMPER STICKER *Wisdom* "For the folks who don't think enough of this country to treat the flag with respect, I say, 'Love it or leave it.'"

117

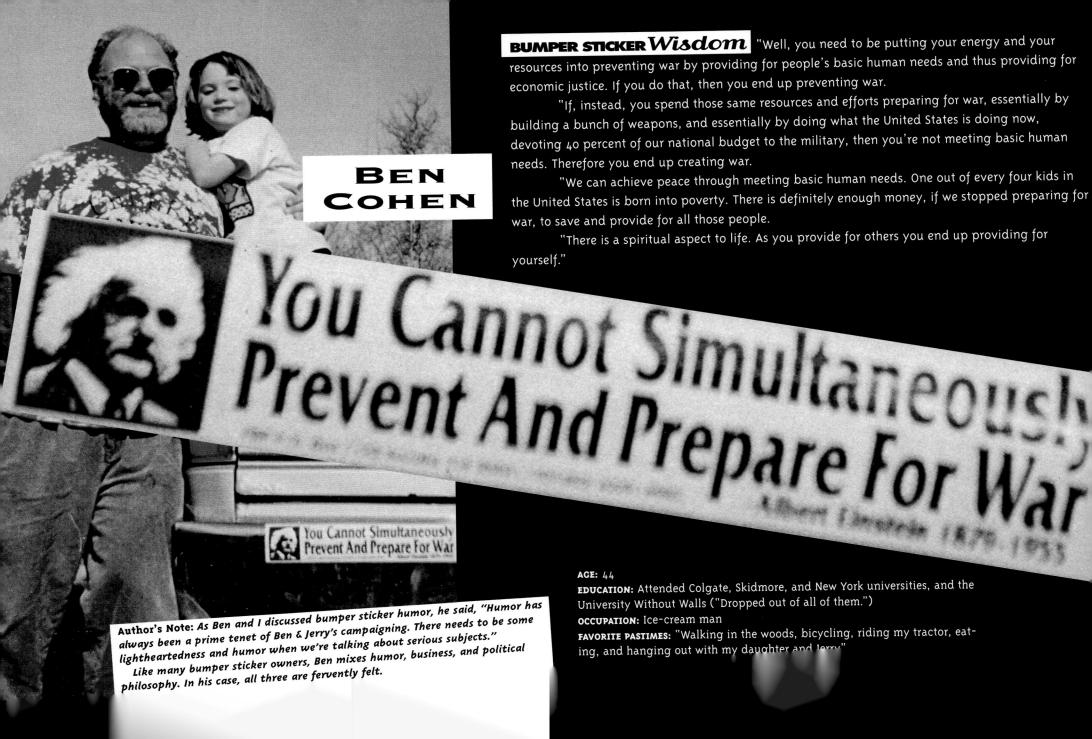

BUMPER STICKER *Wisdom* "Well, you need to be putting your energy and your resources into preventing war by providing for people's basic human needs and thus providing for economic justice. If you do that, then you end up preventing war.

"If, instead, you spend those same resources and efforts preparing for war, essentially by building a bunch of weapons, and essentially by doing what the United States is doing now, devoting 40 percent of our national budget to the military, then you're not meeting basic human needs. Therefore you end up creating war.

"We can achieve peace through meeting basic human needs. One out of every four kids in the United States is born into poverty. There is definitely enough money, if we stopped preparing for war, to save and provide for all those people.

"There is a spiritual aspect to life. As you provide for others you end up providing for yourself."

BEN COHEN

You Cannot Simultaneously Prevent And Prepare For War

You Cannot Simultaneously Prevent And Prepare For War

Author's Note: *As Ben and I discussed bumper sticker humor, he said, "Humor has always been a prime tenet of Ben & Jerry's campaigning. There needs to be some lightheartedness and humor when we're talking about serious subjects."*

Like many bumper sticker owners, Ben mixes humor, business, and political philosophy. In his case, all three are fervently felt.

AGE: 44
EDUCATION: Attended Colgate, Skidmore, and New York universities, and the University Without Walls ("Dropped out of all of them.")
OCCUPATION: Ice-cream man
FAVORITE PASTIMES: "Walking in the woods, bicycling, riding my tractor, eating, and hanging out with my daughter and Jerry"

WENDY KEEDY

AGE: 44
EDUCATION: Lewis and Clark College (French)
OCCUPATION: Mother
FAVORITE PASTIMES: Reading
FAVORITE BOOK: *The Little Prince* by Antoine de Saint-Exupéry
FAVORITE MOVIE: *Saving Grace*
PET PEEVE: People who say "no" and then agree with you

BUMPER STICKER *Wisdom* "I like what the bumper sticker says, and I think it makes people think. A senseless act of beauty that we did was that one time we had our entire basement painted as the secret garden—looking like illustrations from Tasha Tudor's book. So there are gates, birds, bricks, grass, and flowers. I think this bumper sticker was created to make people stop doing random acts of violence and to think, 'Wait, I can do really nice, beautiful, wonderful things just as well as throw bricks through that window.'"

PRACTICE RANDOM KINDNESS & SENSELESS ACTS OF BEAUTY

DONNELLY / COLT CUSTOMSTICKERS, BOX 188, HAMPTON, CT 96247 (203) 455-9621

Author's Note: Wendy's second bumper sticker says "Give peace a chance." She said she made up her own version, "Give pee a chance," and stuck it on her daughter's potty trainer.

STUMPS OF MYSTERY
A WESTERN EXPERIENCE
© Five Percent Left

OREGONEUN
TRANSPLANT

Bucksnort Ti

CROSS-COUNTRY
DRIVE
(REGIONAL)

°MAINE°
BUMPAH
STICKAH
MAINE REGESTRATION STICKAH
°(FOR THE CAH)°
MAINE REGESTRATION STICKAH

Cape Cod
"IT'S THE REAL THING"

HOME OF WORLD CHAMPION COW CHIP THROW
BEAVER, OKLAHOMA

BEAVER OKLA COW CHIP CAPITAL WELCOMES YOU

AGE: 49
EDUCATION: Prairie du Sac High School
OCCUPATION: Scanning coordinator at a Piggly Wiggly supermarket
FAVORITE PASTIMES: Softball, pitching horseshoes, bowling, and shooting pool
FAVORITE BOOK: Reader's Digest condensed books
FAVORITE MOVIE: *Blue Hawaii*
PET PEEVE: Fair-weather friends

BUMPER STICKER *Wisdom*

"It started as a joke when I was the pitcher on a local softball team and one of the other players signed us up for a 'cow-chip throw.' I won, and I've been throwing cow chips ever since. This is my 17th cow-chip throw. I've won the world championship ten times now. I've won the state championship cow-chip throw in Wisconsin eight times."

Author's Note: This was the 25th World Champion Cow Chip Throw, and I convinced a childhood friend of mine to go with me to Beaver, Oklahoma, and to enter the Cow Chip Throw. Beaver, Oklahoma, was Americana at its best—corn dogs, T-shirts, cotton candy, rodeo, and of course, the Cow Chip Throw. I wouldn't have missed it for the world, and, incidentally, my friend placed fourth. Next year she says she wants to go back and win!

KAY HANKINS

TIM SMITH

AGE: 31
EDUCATION: College of the Desert (automotive technology)
OCCUPATION: Mechanic for Goodyear
FAVORITE PASTIMES: Water-skiing
FAVORITE BOOK: *Star Wars* by George Lucas
FAVORITE MOVIE: *Lethal Weapon*
PET PEEVE: Health-insurance companies and paying taxes on top of taxes

Welcome To California Now Go Home

BUMPER STICKER *Wisdom*

"California is getting crowded, and then there's the recession, and it's really bad job-hunting. I wouldn't tell people to come to California at all. It's bad down here right now—earthquakes, riots, and mud slides."

BUMPER STICKER *Wisdom* "It's a lot of work getting a job as an actor. There are so many actors here in Hollywood. I've been looking for acting jobs six to eight months now.

"I was an extra on a TV show, but I'm still trying to get my SAG card [Screen Actors Guild]. The whole process to get your SAG card is almost like a Catch 22, because you have to be on a show with a speaking part, and to be on a show with a speaking part you have to be in the union. What you do is be an extra on every-thing, then network your way into a 'line.'

"I go to interviews and callbacks every day, and I'm studying acting at an acting school. I'm always learning.

"Tourists honk and smile at my bumper sticker. Maybe someone in the movie business will spot it."

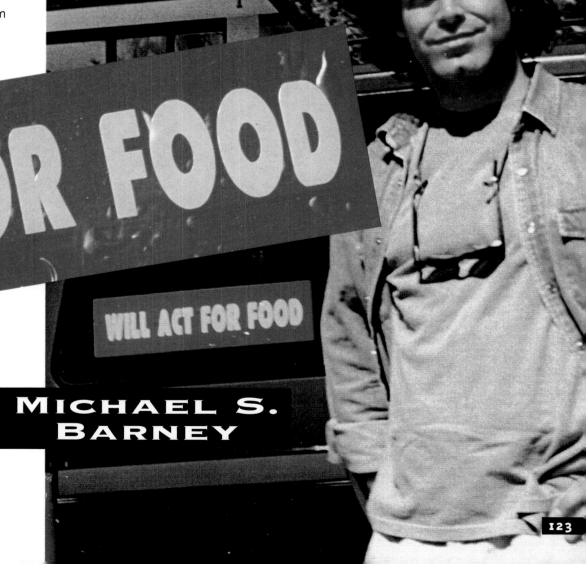

MICHAEL S. BARNEY

AGE: 25

EDUCATION: California State University at Los Angeles (television and film production)

OCCUPATION: Room-service waiter at Chateau Marmont and student of acting

FAVORITE PASTIMES: Sports, exercise, movies, photography, and collecting movie posters

FAVORITE BOOK: *Red Storm Rising* by Tom Clancy

FAVORITE MOVIE: *Star Wars*

PET PEEVE: Los Angeles drivers—"I wish they'd just relax."

"I lived in Kansas eight years before moving west. Life was pretty dull—just go to movies, go to the mall. That's about it. I saw a new movie each week. In Kansas you're just stuck in the middle."

SCOTT YAEGER

AGE: 16
EDUCATION: Catlin Gabel High School
OCCUPATION: Student
FAVORITE PASTIMES: Relaxing—"I got good at it from being in Kansas."
FAVORITE BOOK: *Animal Farm* by George Orwell
FAVORITE MOVIE: *Boyz N the Hood*
PET PEEVE: Annoying repetitiveness

Author's Note: *In my discussion with Scott, he emphasized that his bumper sticker was to be taken humorously, not literally, and he expressed that he is sensitive to the seriousness of suicide.*

SUICIDE IN KANSAS IS REDUNDANT

SUICIDE IN KANSAS IS REDUNDANT

AGE: 32
EDUCATION: Oregon Health Sciences University
OCCUPATION: Dental student
FAVORITE PASTIMES: Skiing, scuba diving, and sailing
FAVORITE BOOK: *The Hobbit* by J.R.R. Tolkien
FAVORITE MOVIE: *Blade Runner*
PET PEEVE: Smokers

MIKE LAWS

BUMPER STICKER *Wisdom* "On the first road trip to Montana, we went to see my brother who was in school there, and we stopped at one of those big tourist-attraction places. I don't know, we always joked with my friends about sheep in Montana, so it was pretty funny to us. I don't know what else—it was just another sticker.

"My brother started putting stickers on this five years ago. It's kind of ongoing. The stickers are holding the car together."

I ♥ LOVE MONTANA

I WANTA GO Baa-aa-ck

Don't mess with Texas

Don't mess with Texas

Author's Note: *Bruce gave me a copy of his book, The Fence. Set in the backwoods of north-central Texas, it is a book of passion, vengeance, and murder. So . . . I wouldn't "mess" with either Bruce McGinnis or Texas, but I sure enjoyed his book.*

BRUCE McGINNIS

AGE: 53
EDUCATION: Hardin-Simmons University (master's) and West Texas A & M (graduate courses in English)
OCCUPATION: Author and professor of English at Amarillo College
FAVORITE PASTIMES: Collecting farm equipment, writing, and collecting Old West memorabilia
FAVORITE BOOK: *Ulysses* by James Joyce
FAVORITE MOVIE: *The Grapes of Wrath*
PET PEEVE: Vulgar-mouthed people and smokers

DOUG PHILLIPS

BUMPER STICKER *Wisdom* "I was actually born in Texas, but with everybody cussing Texans, I liked it and just put it on there."

AGE: 60
EDUCATION: Mobeettie High School
OCCUPATION: Heavy-equipment operator and race-horse breeder
FAVORITE PASTIMES: Roping and going to the horse races
FAVORITE BOOK: Westerns by Zane Grey
FAVORITE MOVIE: *Lonesome Dove*
PET PEEVE: None

127

BUMPER STICKER *Wisdom* "I got the bumper sticker from the Sons of the Confederate Veterans. My wife has one on her car that says 'Heritage not hate,' which is really the true meaning.

"Certain segments of society use the battle flag as a hate sign. For example, the Klu Klux Klan uses it. They're not authorized to use the flag, and they were no part of the Confederate movement, then or now.

"The outlaw motorcycle clubs and the young Nazis have used the battle flag as a symbol, but that isn't what it was for.

"It just means, I was Southern-born and -bred. All those folks who have a Southern ancestry should work to preserve that heritage. It's something worth preserving. It's part of history."

WILLIAM C. RUDDOCK

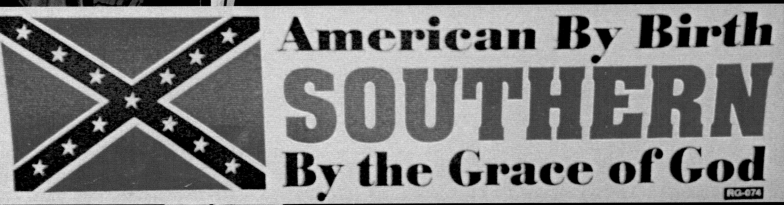

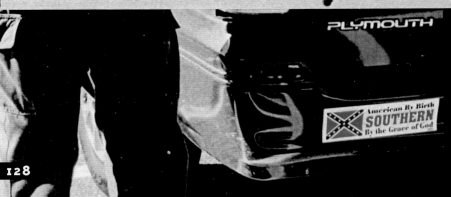

AGE: 65

EDUCATION: Vail Institute (engineering)

OCCUPATION: Executive director of the Confederate Library (genealogical library and research center)

FAVORITE PASTIMES: Travel and music (playing drums for the J.E.B. Stuart Band)

FAVORITE BOOK: *Yankee Autumn in Acadiana* by David C. Edmonds

FAVORITE MOVIE: *Gettysburg*

PET PEEVE: People who pay no attention to business hours

DAVID PATRICK KELLEY

AGE: 24
EDUCATION: Weymouth South High School
OCCUPATION: Radiator mechanic
FAVORITE PASTIMES: Travel
FAVORITE BOOK: *Trinity* by Leon Uris
FAVORITE MOVIE: *In the Name of the Father*
PET PEEVE: People who criticize the opinions of others

ENGLAND GET OUT OF IRELAND

BUMPER STICKER *Wisdom* "I was at a Wolftones concert—they're the most popular band out of Ireland—and I saw this sticker and bought it because it's directly to the point. I had a couple of people try to peel it off because they didn't agree with it.

"Ireland is just this tiny little country, but England wants to dominate everything. England is either greedy or stubborn. People shouldn't have to live with armored cars and tanks and guys walking around with M-16s. That's why we kicked England out of Boston 200 years ago.

"It's a dispute between the Catholics and the Protestants. Primarily, southern Ireland is Catholic, and northern Ireland and England are Protestant. So it's not just a territorial dispute. It's a religious war, a holy war.

"The Irish flag is green, white, and orange. The green stands for the Catholics, the white means peace, and the orange means Protestant. In 1916, when Ireland became independent, they made this flag with the intention that there be peace. The goal for the Irish people, either Protestant or Catholic, is just to have peace."

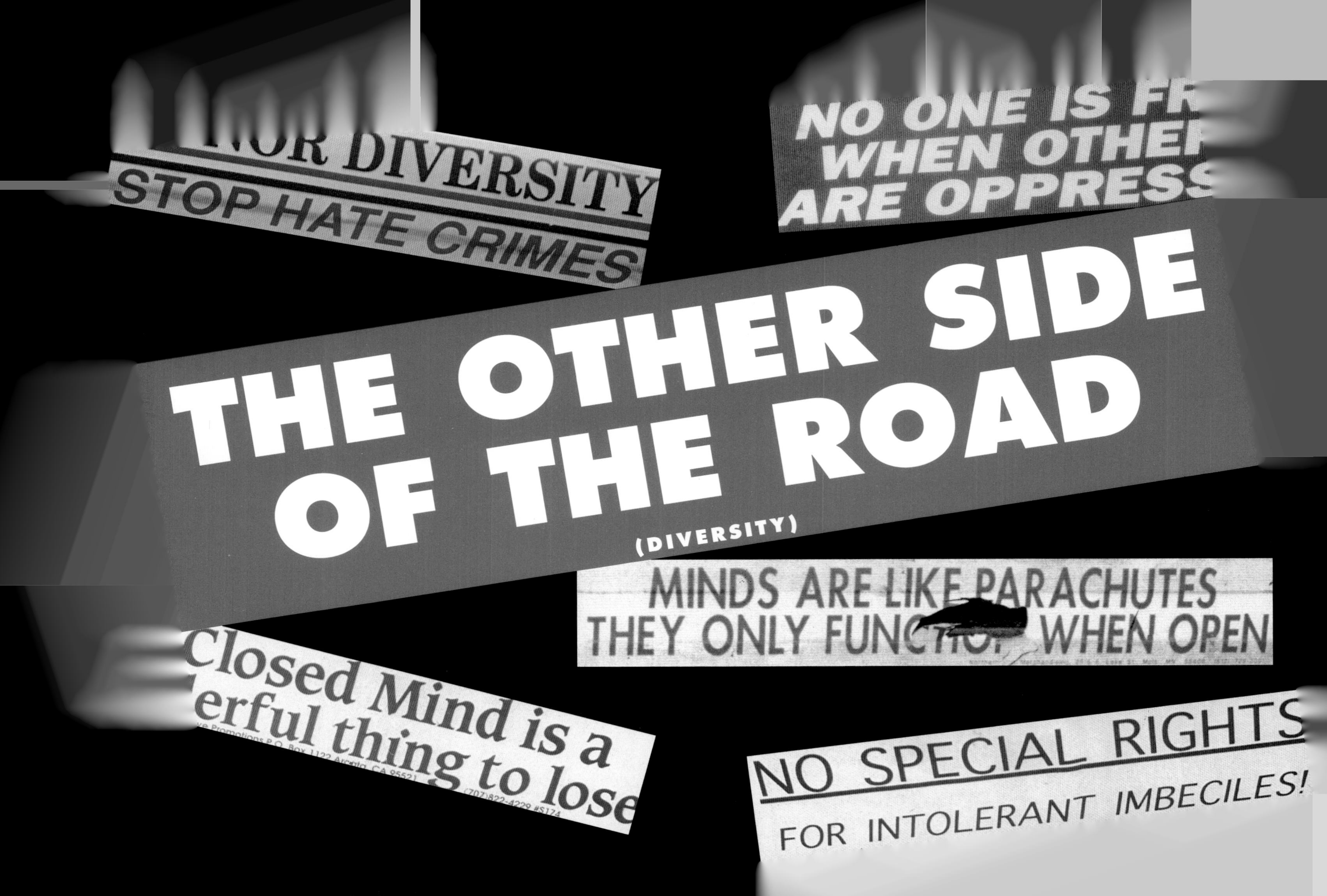
NOR DIVERSITY
STOP HATE CRIMES
NO ONE IS FR
WHEN OTHE
ARE OPPRESS
THE OTHER SIDE
OF THE ROAD
(DIVERSITY)
MINDS ARE LIKE PARACHUTES
THEY ONLY FUNC WHEN OPEN
Closed Mind is a
erful thing to lose
ve Promotions P.O. Box 1122 Arcata, CA 95521 (707)822-4229 #S174
NO SPECIAL RIGHTS
FOR INTOLERANT IMBECILES!

PATRICIA NEILSEN

AGE: 46
EDUCATION: Mount Hood Community College (speech)
OCCUPATION: Accessibility-programs manager for public transportation
FAVORITE PASTIMES: Working and reading
FAVORITE BOOK: Books by Danielle Steele
FAVORITE MOVIE: *The Graduate*
PET PEEVE: People who make assumptions before getting to know you

The only true handicap is people's ATTITUDES!

© 1992 Moving Forward Newspaper, Torrance, CA - 1 John 4:7

The only true handicap is people's ATTITUDES!

BUMPER STICKER *Wisdom* "I am a person who has lived with a disability for over 30 years. I believe attitude is the biggest barrier for persons with disabilities, or actually any kind of diversity-related issue. Attitudes are the real disability. The bumper sticker delivers the right kind of message."

ELIZABETH BISHOP

AGE: 50
EDUCATION: Bowling Green State University (Ph.D. in American culture and Native studies)
OCCUPATION: Professor at Navajo Community College
FAVORITE PASTIMES: Dancing, networking, reading, and writing
FAVORITE BOOK: *The Cherokee Alphabet*
FAVORITE MOVIE: *What's Eating Gilbert Grape*
PET PEEVE: "Robotal" people

BUMPER STICKER *Wisdom* "My two bumper stickers go together, saying ecology. They're saying, there was something once, and now what happened? It's hard to find what it was then. You could put it in these words: Where you were then, you might be now. So why not be what you might have been, and just be—sort of the celebration at the time of creation. I wouldn't take one bumper sticker without the other."

NATIVE AMERICANS DISCOVERED AMERICA

NATIVE AMER
DISCOVERED A

good planets are hard to find

AGE: 53
EDUCATION: University of Washington (Ph.D. in higher education), Rutgers (MSW), and University of Washington (political science)
OCCUPATION: Director of the Chemawa Alcohol Education Center
FAVORITE PASTIMES: Bull riding, rugby, and triathlons
FAVORITE BOOK: *Never Cry Wolf* by Farley Mowat
FAVORITE MOVIE: *Casablanca*
PET PEEVE: "People who don't walk their talk, especially right-wing flag-wavers who don't truly believe in equal justice and equal opportunity for everybody"

JOHN SPENCE

YOU ARE ON INDIAN LAND

BUMPER STICKER *Wisdom* "I look back at the bumper stickers I've had. The first was 'Custer wore an Arrow shirt.' Someone gave it to me, and I got some negative reactions to it in Montana.

"Then I had the AA bumper sticker 'Easy does it' on my car because I've been involved with Alcoholics Anonymous for 12 years now.

"With the bumper sticker 'You are on Indian land,' I've had several reactions. For example, a guy I work with saw some cats on my car and told me he chased them off because they were on Indian land. Then I saw a couple of Japanese exchange students pointing at the bumper sticker and laughing. I thought, 'Well, this is good. They know something is going on.' The latest reaction was last week when I was at a meeting and these two Indian guys came up to me and said they wanted bumper stickers just like it."

SHARIE SMITH

AGE: 30
EDUCATION: Portland State University (psychology and social science)
OCCUPATION: Owner of "Vintage Re Vu" (a vintage clothing store) and an extra in local movie productions
FAVORITE PASTIMES: Creating candelabras, vegging out in front of the television, biking, walking, and going to movies
FAVORITE BOOK: *The Seven Habits of Highly Effective People* by Stephen R. Covey
FAVORITE MOVIE: *A Streetcar Named Desire*
PET PEEVE: "Not being able to have a great man to share my life with"

BUMPER STICKER *Wisdom* "I should tell you that the first bumper sticker I printed was 'Abolish apartheid.' I was in college and learning a lot about apartheid in South Africa and about Nelson Mandela. I started selling them out of a little box, sitting on the ground at Saturday Market. I also sold them at college, and they kept paying for themselves. I've sold about two or three thousand. Now you can buy them in record stores.

"With 'Racism sucks,' I was still in college, and at the time I was learning about African-American history, African history, and just understanding and knowing the facts about racism. I went to look for a bumper sticker like this, and nothing was available. There were similar stickers like 'No racism' and 'Honor diversity,' but I wanted something a little stronger. So, I just decided to go with 'Racism sucks.' I liked it so much that I decided to print them up and make stickers and T-shirts.

"As to people's reactions, I've had everything from 'Right on, I've got to have one' to 'I hate *sucks*.' One woman came up to me and said, '*Sucks* sucks!'"

MARION CLAIR

AGE: 49
EDUCATION: Antioch University (Seattle)
(master's in psychology and counseling)
OCCUPATION: Educator and teacher of
English as a second language
FAVORITE PASTIMES: Tennis
FAVORITE BOOK: *Men Are from Mars, Women
Are from Venus* by John Gray
FAVORITE MOVIE: *The Wizard of Oz*
PET PEEVE: Freeway traffic in Seattle

The first Boat People were White

PHRESH STICKERS (503) 285-6539

986·DJI

The first Boat People
were White

BUMPER STICKER *Wisdom* "I'm trying to tell people they should think twice before categorizing refugees and people from other countries that come into this country. Not that I don't think there should be some legitimate restrictions and qualifications for entering, but to just have a blanket, negative reaction to anyone whose families haven't lived here for 200 years isn't right. They should think again about where their ancestors came from. My ancestors came over on a boat. Nobody complained about them. Once we accept people into this country, they should be embraced."

Author's Note: Marion's bumper sticker has confused some people who took it as a racist statement—not Marion's intent at all. She finally had to take it off her car.

ROLAND BAYSE

AGE: 32
EDUCATION: Diamond High School
OCCUPATION: Student of cosmetology and seeking work as a professional model
FAVORITE PASTIMES: Dancing, nature hikes, road trips, and exercise
FAVORITE BOOK: *The Little Prince* by Antoine de Saint-Exupéry and *The Vampire Lestat* by Anne Rice
FAVORITE MOVIE: *Priscilla, Queen of the Desert*
PET PEEVE: "Other people's control issues over my life"

BUMPER STICKER *Wisdom* "I think there are a lot of bumper stickers out there that are corny, but with this one it is a corny approach to a serious issue. It's a very 'in your face' approach to 'coming out.' I think it gives people like me the message that they need to stop being 'in the closet,' because we're not going to get respect and equality by being quiet about who we are. The message it gives to the people who dislike me is, 'Look, I don't care what you think about me. We're queer and we're here, so get used to it.'"

THE MARINES ARE LOOKING FOR A FEW GOOD MEN...SO AM I!

AGE: 42
EDUCATION: Missouri Western State College (business)
OCCUPATION: Formerly a technical worker for an oil company
FAVORITE PASTIMES: Photography, handguns, bike riding, dogs (rottweilers), and movies
FAVORITE BOOK: Newspapers and *People* magazine
FAVORITE MOVIE: *The Blues Brothers*
PET PEEVE: People who drive slow in the passing lane on the highway

Keep the Queens Out of the Marines

BUMPER STICKER *Wisdom* "I bought the bumper sticker at a local gun show about a month ago. I saw it and I was browsing and I had to walk past it and think about it about three or four times. It probably took me 15 to 20 minutes to finally decide to go ahead and buy it. I don't think gays should be in the military in an open fashion. You know, they should definitely be in the closet. I know that if, I'm not gay, but if I were gay and I found myself in the military for whatever reason, the last thing that I would do would be to announce to everybody that I was gay. There's a lot of anti-gay and anti-lesbian sentiment within the military, and I would also fear for that person's well-being, for the gay or lesbian person, you know. I think, too, they're bad for morale within the military unit they're in. It impacts that negatively. I never served in the military. My oldest brother, who is now deceased, served in the Marine Corps. He had two tours in Vietnam. I have two little brothers who also served—one in the Navy and one in the Army."

Author's Note: *Sutton's wife, Lisa, doesn't like his bumper sticker and told him she won't ride in his car until he takes it off.*

SHIRLEY BROTHERS

BUMPER STICKER *Wisdom* "I got the bumper sticker because a friend of mine is HIV-positive. He is still healthy. He looks great. He got it through a blood transfusion. It's a very personal matter to me.

"I don't think there is enough being done, because AIDS is still perceived as a gay disease. It's not anymore. I'm concerned about educating the next generation. When you are a teenager you think you are invincible. Nature is nature, and they are going to experiment.

"There is a great support group down here in Provincetown, Massachusetts."

FIGHT AIDS NOT PEOPLE WITH AIDS

DONNELLY/COLT CUSTOM PRINTING BOX 188 HAMPTON, CONN. 00247

FIGHT AIDS NOT PEOPLE WITH AIDS

AGE: 44
EDUCATION: Champlain College (business management)
OCCUPATION: Chemical and dye sales representative for the textile industry
FAVORITE PASTIMES: Anything outdoors, walking on the beach, clamming, and gardening
FAVORITE BOOK: *Kon-Tiki* by Thor Heyerdahl
FAVORITE MOVIE: *And the Band Played On*
PET PEEVE: "How greedy society has become. Everything has become money and power."

HUMOR
Never leave home
without it.

Beam me up Scotty
There's no intelligent life down here

THE LONG AND WINDING ROAD

(MISCELLANEOUS)

EVEN PARANOIDS HAVE ENEMIES

HELP ME FIND MY GROUP
'M THEIR LEADER

COMPOST HAPPENS

© 1993 NORTHERN SUN MERCHANDISING (612)729-2001

BRIAN BELMONTE

AGE: 33
EDUCATION: Greenfield Community College (liberal arts)
OCCUPATION: Musician
FAVORITE PASTIMES: Golf, skiing,and drum circles (a jam session involving only drummers)
FAVORITE BOOK: *Moon the Loon: The Rock and Roll Life of Keith Moon* by Dougal Butler
FAVORITE MOVIE: *The Pope of Greenwich Village*
PET PEEVE: People who say "no"

LONG LIVE THE KING!

BUMPER STICKER *Wisdom* "I've always wanted to go to Graceland ever since I can remember.

"After I saw that U2 came here and recorded at one of the studios, that gave me the OK that it was really cool. I had to come here.

"I have a lot of memories of Elvis when I was growing up. Coming here resurrected Elvis.

"'Long live the King!' means he's always in my heart. He was the man that basically started rock and roll, and that's what I do for a living now.

"He *is* the King.

"He *is* the Granddaddy."

Author's Note: I waited several hours in the parking lot at Graceland for Brian to return to his car. The wait was worth it. He is a true fan.

AGE: 26

EDUCATION: Brown University (psychology)

OCCUPATION: Director of children's books for a publishing company

FAVORITE PASTIMES: Playing pool, snowboarding, rafting, writing children's stories, reading, camping, and playing with kids

FAVORITE BOOK: *Hope for the Flowers* by Trina Paulus, "plus all the amazing children's books my company does, of course"

FAVORITE MOVIE: *Thelma and Louise* and *Harold and Maude*

PET PEEVE: People who talk but don't listen, and people who think they know everything

MICHELLE ROEHM

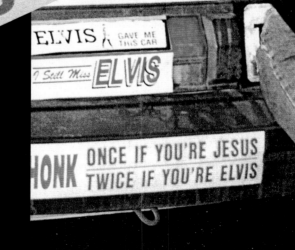

BUMPER STICKER *Wisdom* "I'm actually not *that* into Elvis— I mean I like his music and I think he was a pretty decent guy, but what I'm really interested in is the cult of Elvis—the people who are totally obsessed. If you've ever been to Graceland you know what I'm talking about. There are people there who are seriously having a religious experience. I once met an Elvis impersonator at Graceland who had brought his two-year-old daughter with him to see the home of the King. He was definitely making a pilgrimage to his own personal Mecca. The place is filled with people like that.

"Also, there are actually lots of Jesus-Elvis parallels. Both died young, both were painted on black velvet, both loved peanut butter and banana sandwiches—just kidding. I get a lot of response to the bumper sticker. Mostly people drive by laughing, but a lot of people honk too. I love the people who honk twice—I mean if you think you're Elvis, more power to you. But the people who honk just once kind of freak me out. A lot of people honk three times and think they're really funny. Ha-ha. It gets kind of old after about the millionth time!"

HONK ONCE IF YOU'RE JESUS TWICE IF YOU'RE ELVIS

AGE: 31

EDUCATION: David Lipscomb College (government and public administration)

OCCUPATION: Group sales manager, Opryland USA

FAVORITE PASTIMES: Rifle, bow, and black-powder hunting

FAVORITE BOOK: *The Way Things Ought to Be* by Rush Limbaugh

FAVORITE MOVIE: *Gone with the Wind*

PET PEEVE: "People who I can't trust"

W. CLARK ALLEN

BUMPER STICKER *Wisdom* "'Country 'Til I Die' was John Anderson's latest release, and a friend of mine gave me the bumper sticker. I liked it and put it on my truck. I don't listen to anything other than country music.

"I've lived three miles from Opryland most of my life, and I work there now. The best part of working at Opryland are the people who visit. When they get here they've saved up all year or a couple of years, and they've loaded up the truck and come to Opryland. They're all ready to go. It's exciting to see those folks."

MONTY FISHER

AGE: 48
EDUCATION: Willamette High School
OCCUPATION: Carpenter and jack-of-all-trades
FAVORITE PASTIMES: "Playing with my son and writing country folk music"
FAVORITE BOOK: *Treasure Island* by Robert Louis Stevenson
FAVORITE MOVIE: *High Sierra*
PET PEEVE: People who take advantage of people's goodness and people who don't know "Jack Shit"

BUMPER STICKER *Wisdom*   "'Jack Shit' is wisdom and 'Jack Shit' is common sense. For example, if you want a horse to get in a trailer, you put something in the trailer the horse wants.

"To make it in life, you have to know 'Jack Shit,' and I want to pass 'Jack Shit' on to my son.

"As a matter of fact, I think it would be good if the president knew 'Jack Shit.'"

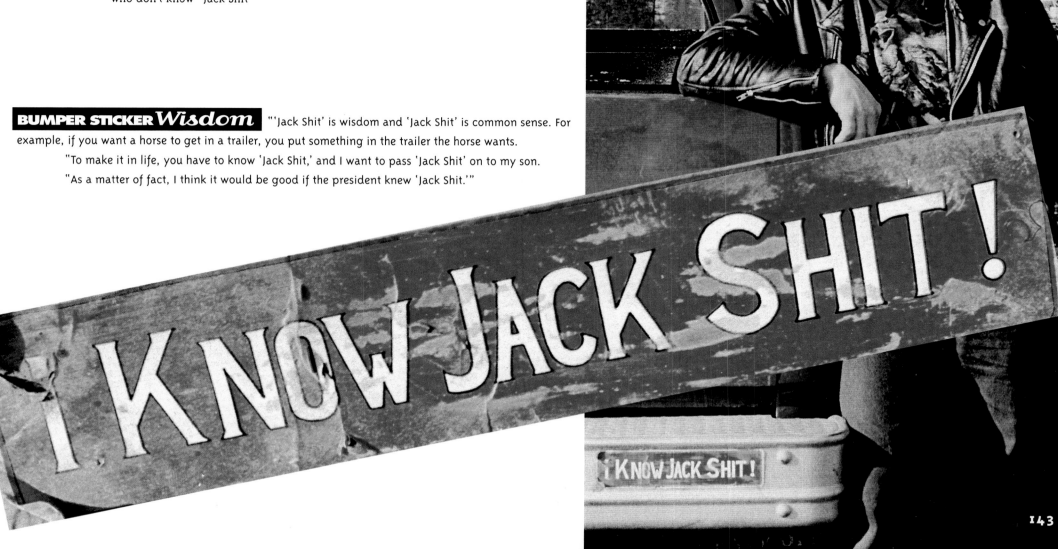

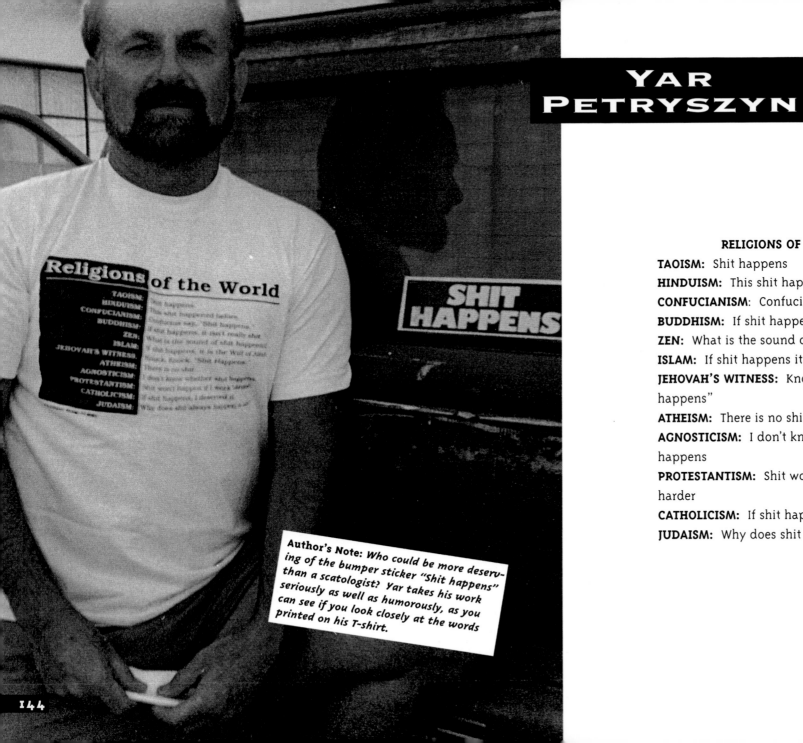

YAR PETRYSZYN

RELIGIONS OF THE WORLD

TAOISM: Shit happens

HINDUISM: This shit happened before

CONFUCIANISM: Confucius say "Shit happens"

BUDDHISM: If shit happens, it really isn't shit

ZEN: What is the sound of shit happening?

ISLAM: If shit happens it is the will of Allah

JEHOVAH'S WITNESS: Knock, knock, "Shit happens"

ATHEISM: There is no shit

AGNOSTICISM: I don't know whether shit happens

PROTESTANTISM: Shit won't happen if I work harder

CATHOLICISM: If shit happens, I deserved it

JUDAISM: Why does shit always happen to us?

Author's Note: Who could be more deserving of the bumper sticker "Shit happens" than a scatologist? Yar takes his work seriously as well as humorously, as you can see if you look closely at the words printed on his T-shirt.

AGE: 49
EDUCATION: University of Arizona (Ph.D. in ecological and evolutionary biology)
OCCUPATION: Scatologist and assistant curator of the mammal collection at the University of Arizona
FAVORITE PASTIMES: Scuba diving, poetry, hiking, pottery, and painting
FAVORITE BOOK: Science-fiction books
FAVORITE MOVIE: "Movies are not that important to me."
PET PEEVE: People who are late

BUMPER STICKER _Wisdom_ "One of my scientific and personal interests is scatology, which is just a fancy name for poop. Being a biologist and interested in the natural world around us, especially animals of different sorts, often you don't see animals because they are nocturnal or secretive. But they always leave their calling card. So you can, with a little bit of knowledge, tell what's out there, approximately how many have been running around, and what they have been eating. Scats tell you something about the condition of their habitat. There's a lot of information in poop."

BUMPER STICKER *Wisdom* "My favorite aunt lived in Atlanta, Georgia, for a couple years, and I visited her the summer of '88. At the time the Georgia Legislature and the Louisiana Legislature were trying to get a bill passed where you couldn't have obscene words more than one-quarter of an inch in height on a bumper sticker. They were trying to get all obscene words off bumper stickers. In Georgia we came across this bumper sticker, 'Doo-doo occurs,' and I've had it ever since and it's been real fun."

CASSANDRA DOVER

DOO-DOO OCCURS

Compliments of SUN/SOUTH Development Corporation 404-393-9993

AGE: 34
EDUCATION: University of New Orleans (English)
OCCUPATION: Assistant court librarian and CEO of the World Famous Irish Channel Ironworks
FAVORITE PASTIMES: Renovating houses, bike riding, and getting projects done
FAVORITE BOOK: *The Hobbit* by J.R.R. Tolkien
FAVORITE MOVIE: *An Affair to Remember*
PET PEEVE: Impoliteness

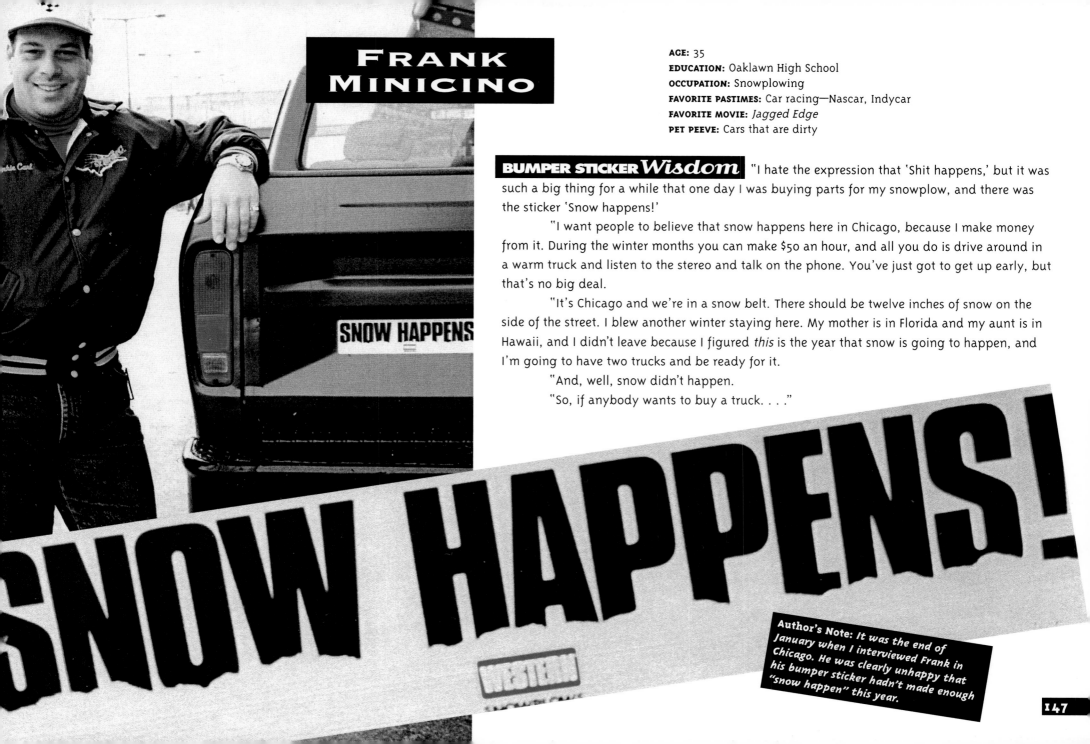

FRANK MINICINO

AGE: 35
EDUCATION: Oaklawn High School
OCCUPATION: Snowplowing
FAVORITE PASTIMES: Car racing—Nascar, Indycar
FAVORITE MOVIE: *Jagged Edge*
PET PEEVE: Cars that are dirty

BUMPER STICKER *Wisdom*   "I hate the expression that 'Shit happens,' but it was such a big thing for a while that one day I was buying parts for my snowplow, and there was the sticker 'Snow happens!'

"I want people to believe that snow happens here in Chicago, because I make money from it. During the winter months you can make $50 an hour, and all you do is drive around in a warm truck and listen to the stereo and talk on the phone. You've just got to get up early, but that's no big deal.

"It's Chicago and we're in a snow belt. There should be twelve inches of snow on the side of the street. I blew another winter staying here. My mother is in Florida and my aunt is in Hawaii, and I didn't leave because I figured *this* is the year that snow is going to happen, and I'm going to have two trucks and be ready for it.

"And, well, snow didn't happen.

"So, if anybody wants to buy a truck. . . ."

SNOW HAPPENS

SNOW HAPPENS!

Author's Note: It was the end of January when I interviewed Frank in Chicago. He was clearly unhappy that his bumper sticker hadn't made enough "snow happen" this year.

PHRED BISHOP

AGE: 36

EDUCATION: Mount Hood Community College (forestry technology)

OCCUPATION: Owner of Phresh Stickers from Phresh Ideas

FAVORITE PASTIMES: Playing music, watching movies, and taking lines out of movies and making bumper stickers out of them

FAVORITE BOOK: *Star Wars* by George Lucas

FAVORITE MOVIE: *Fear of a Black Hat*

PET PEEVE: People who drive fast and have bumper stickers that say "For kids sake, slow down"

BUMPER STICKER *Wisdom* "I was printing T-shirts for Nike, and one day I saw these bumper stickers and said to myself, 'I can do that.' I had all these 'phresh' ideas like 'If Elvis was still alive, he'd be dead by now,' and so I just started printing them. Now I have about 153 bumper stickers I sell in my store, Phresh Ideas.

"My wife came up with the idea for 'Fahrfenäked,' or she saw it somewhere and said, 'We've got to do that.' It's a continuation of Volkswagen's 'Fahrvergnügen' and the other takeoff bumper sticker 'Fukengrüven.'

"I also have on my van, 'I'm not a bum, my wife works.' Actually, we have five kids and we work really hard.

"The kinds of people who buy bumper stickers are very diverse. There

Fahrfenäked

are people who come in and are not very well off. They'll buy a couple of stickers. On the other hand, people in suits and people from other states and from other countries buy our stickers. We have a guy from Utah who calls and has me print stickers they won't print in Utah, like 'Everyone in Utah is a third cousin once removed.' He also did one that said 'Don't trust anyone under 5,000 feet.'

"My wife is into pagan bumper stickers. She did 'Christians, can't live with them, can't throw them to the lions anymore.'

"When I get ideas I usually just scribble them on napkins. When I have a bunch, I print 'em up."

SIMON GARCIA

AGE: 20

EDUCATION: University of Arkansas at Little Rock (architecture)

OCCUPATION: Clerk

FAVORITE PASTIMES: Drawing or doing tattoos

FAVORITE BOOK: *The Eyes of the Dragon* by Stephen King

FAVORITE MOVIE: *The Hunt for Red October*

PET PEEVE: People slowing down as they get on the highway

BUMPER STICKER *Wisdom* "I love music. I like to listen to music all the time, and any time I'm going anywhere I'm just 'Fukengrüven.' It's a takeoff on 'Fahrvergnügen,' which means *ecstasy*. That's just why I had to have the bumper sticker."

Author's Note: *This...*

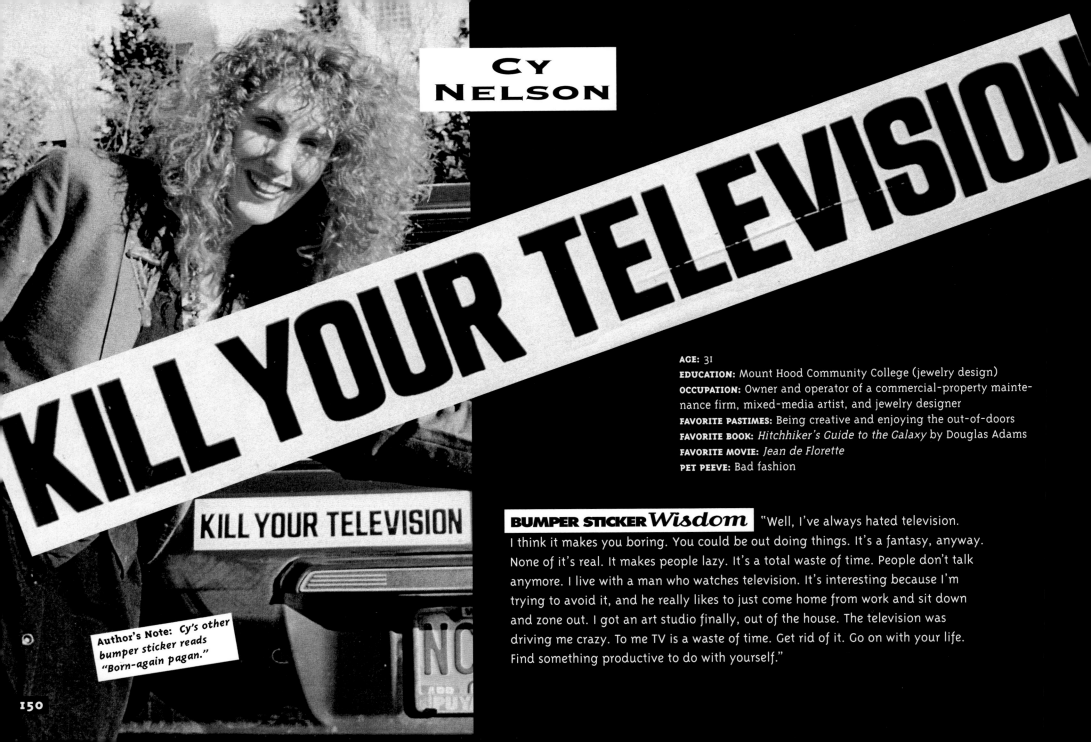

CY NELSON

KILL YOUR TELEVISION

AGE: 31
EDUCATION: Mount Hood Community College (jewelry design)
OCCUPATION: Owner and operator of a commercial-property maintenance firm, mixed-media artist, and jewelry designer
FAVORITE PASTIMES: Being creative and enjoying the out-of-doors
FAVORITE BOOK: *Hitchhiker's Guide to the Galaxy* by Douglas Adams
FAVORITE MOVIE: *Jean de Florette*
PET PEEVE: Bad fashion

BUMPER STICKER *Wisdom* "Well, I've always hated television. I think it makes you boring. You could be out doing things. It's a fantasy, anyway. None of it's real. It makes people lazy. It's a total waste of time. People don't talk anymore. I live with a man who watches television. It's interesting because I'm trying to avoid it, and he really likes to just come home from work and sit down and zone out. I got an art studio finally, out of the house. The television was driving me crazy. To me TV is a waste of time. Get rid of it. Go on with your life. Find something productive to do with yourself."

KILL YOUR TELEVISION

Author's Note: Cy's other bumper sticker reads "Born-again pagan."

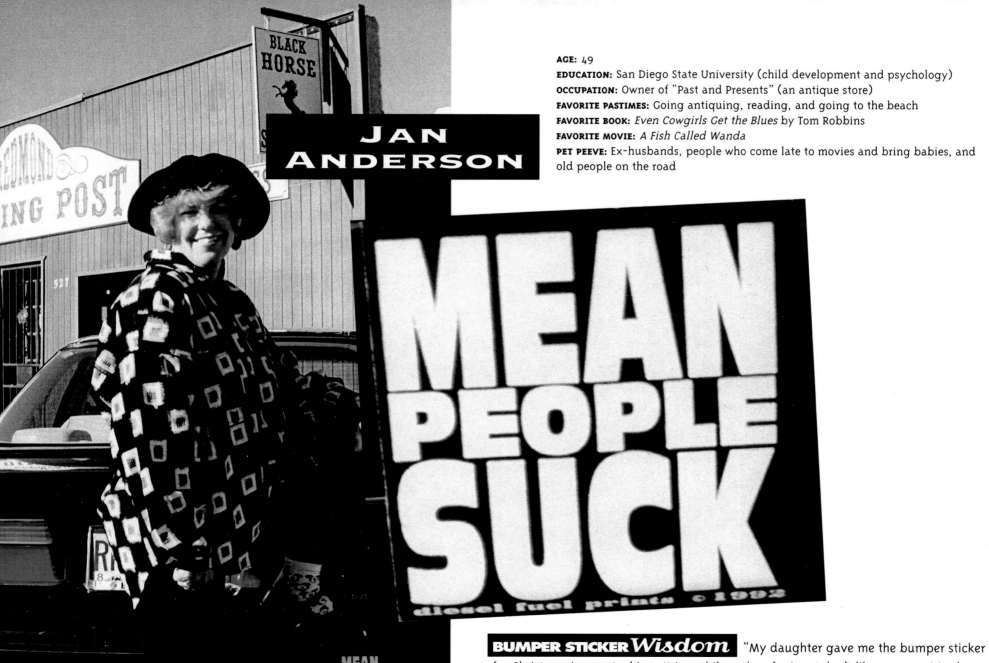

JAN ANDERSON

AGE: 49
EDUCATION: San Diego State University (child development and psychology)
OCCUPATION: Owner of "Past and Presents" (an antique store)
FAVORITE PASTIMES: Going antiquing, reading, and going to the beach
FAVORITE BOOK: *Even Cowgirls Get the Blues* by Tom Robbins
FAVORITE MOVIE: *A Fish Called Wanda*
PET PEEVE: Ex-husbands, people who come late to movies and bring babies, and old people on the road

MEAN PEOPLE SUCK

diesel fuel prints © 1992

BUMPER STICKER *Wisdom* "My daughter gave me the bumper sticker for Christmas in my stocking. It is a philosophy of mine. I don't like mean-spirited people. I can be one occasionally, but it's not really me. The meanest person I know is my first ex-husband. Or my second ex-husband's present wife. Gotcha!"

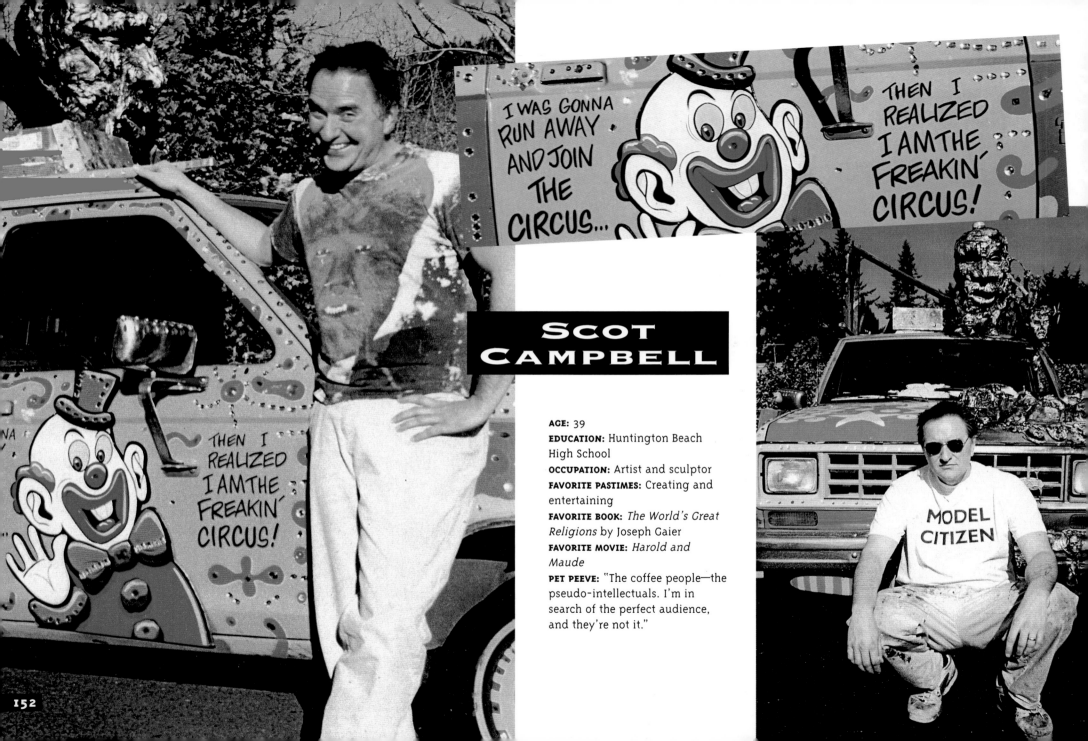

I WAS GONNA RUN AWAY AND JOIN THE CIRCUS...

THEN I REALIZED I AM THE FREAKIN' CIRCUS!

THEN I REALIZED I AM THE FREAKIN' CIRCUS!

SCOT CAMPBELL

AGE: 39

EDUCATION: Huntington Beach High School

OCCUPATION: Artist and sculptor

FAVORITE PASTIMES: Creating and entertaining

FAVORITE BOOK: *The World's Great Religions* by Joseph Gaier

FAVORITE MOVIE: *Harold and Maude*

PET PEEVE: "The coffee people—the pseudo-intellectuals. I'm in search of the perfect audience, and they're not it."

MODEL CITIZEN

THIS IS POLITICALLY CORRECT... MY HOME PLANET!

DON'T WORRY... GOD KNOWS IT'S ON THE ROAD!

BUMPER STICKER Wisdom "I saw a girl with a shirt that actually said, 'I am going to run away and join the circus,' and I thought that's kind of neat, and then I thought, but I am the freakin' circus. I painted it on the door of my truck that same day. It's really true. It's like everything is inside of me. I will be an actor, a singer, a musician, a dancer, a sculptor, an artist. I don't have to run away and join the circus. It's all here, all the excitement, the fun. I am the circus.

"There are a lot of reasons my car has two sides. One, I probably do it for some subconscious reason that I don't know of, because my last car looked like this too.

"My car is like a yin-and-yang thing. I think everybody has in them the potential to be quite cruel and evil, and they have the potential to be quite good and saintly. They can go either way. So there's that sort of idea.

"It's also the idea that it's just funny. The main reason is the contrast and the humor. It gets me a lot of recognition. It's so weird. On the one side you have this evil, twisted, 'Freddie's nightmare' lookin' thing, and the other side looks like an advertisement for some day-care center."

Author's Note: Scot and his car are hard to miss. His two-sided, good/bad, schizophrenic car carries many messages, and though not your typical bumper sticker genre, I felt he deserved a place in Bumper Sticker Wisdom.

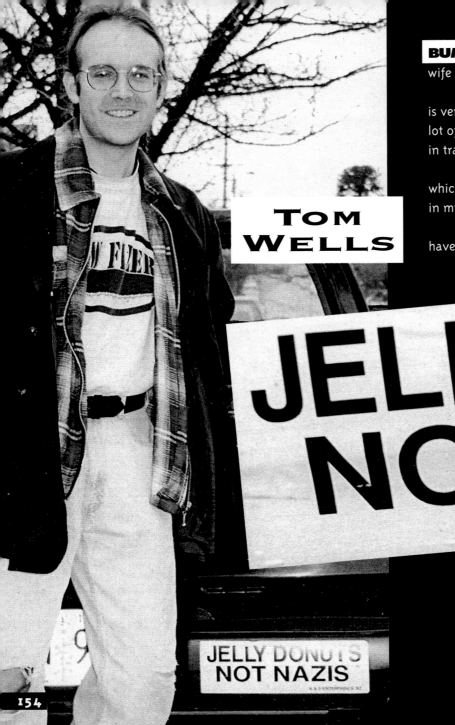

BUMPER STICKER *Wisdom* "'Jelly donuts—not Nazis' was a piece of graffiti on a wall my wife saw, and I have to give her credit for having the genius to put it on a bumper sticker.

"I put it on my car because I like the dialectic of a jelly donut and a Nazi. One is very silly and one is very evil. I also like the fact that it is a Dada statement in that it means absolutely nothing and means a lot of things at the same time. It makes people wonder, and I get a lot of strange reactions. People stop me in traffic and ask me about it.

"There is an interesting theory because Kennedy went to Germany and said, 'Ich bin ein Berliner,' which translates, 'I am a jelly donut.' [Kennedy should have said, 'Ich bin Berliner,' meaning, 'I am a Berliner in my spirit.'] So, there is that connection.

"But basically I like the diametric opposites of the silliness and the absolute evilness. That's why I have it on my car. Otherwise I would never have any other bumper sticker."

TOM WELLS

JELLY DONUTS NOT NAZIS

K & S ENTERPRISES '92

AGE: 31
EDUCATION: Appalachian State University
OCCUPATION: Biologist for the Primate Center
FAVORITE PASTIMES: Music and ultimate frisbee
FAVORITE BOOK: *Trout Fishing in America, The Pill Versus the Spring Hill Mine Disaster and in Watermelon Sugar* by Richard Brautigan
FAVORITE MOVIE: *Raging Bull*
PET PEEVE: Hypocritical people

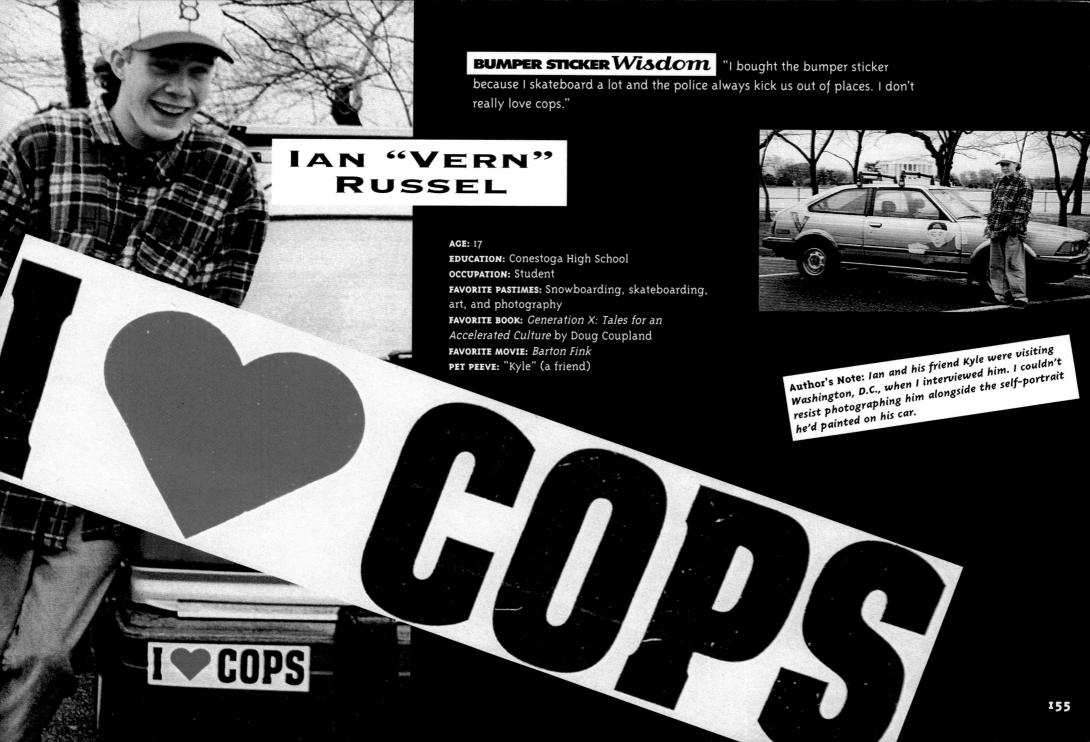

BUMPER STICKER *Wisdom* "I bought the bumper sticker because I skateboard a lot and the police always kick us out of places. I don't really love cops."

IAN "VERN" RUSSEL

AGE: 17
EDUCATION: Conestoga High School
OCCUPATION: Student
FAVORITE PASTIMES: Snowboarding, skateboarding, art, and photography
FAVORITE BOOK: *Generation X: Tales for an Accelerated Culture* by Doug Coupland
FAVORITE MOVIE: *Barton Fink*
PET PEEVE: "Kyle" (a friend)

Author's Note: Ian and his friend Kyle were visiting Washington, D.C., when I interviewed him. I couldn't resist photographing him alongside the self-portrait he'd painted on his car.

I ♥ COPS

I ♥ COPS

ANDREA PATTERSON

AGE: 19
EDUCATION: Portland Community College at Rock Creek
OCCUPATION: Student
FAVORITE PASTIMES: Hiking, writing poetry, and going to movies
FAVORITE BOOK: *Watchers* by Dean Koontz
FAVORITE MOVIE: *Stand by Me*
PET PEEVE: "Everything my mother does"

BUMPER STICKER *Wisdom* "I thought this bumper sticker was one everyone could relate to. It was fun. There are so many depressing things you could put on your car, like 'Stop apartheid.' When I see bumper stickers like that I'm like, yeah, are they really going to go to South Africa and help out if someone asks them? And well, this bumper sticker is just honest."

HONK
IF YOU HATE YOUR HAIR, TOO

BUMPER STICKER *Wisdom* "What I don't like about being diabetic are the shots, and I wish they'd come up with a cure. Yeah, too much sugar also makes some kids hyper. It's probably healthy for all people to eat less sugar."

AGE: 8
EDUCATION: Three Rivers School
OCCUPATION: Student
FAVORITE PASTIMES: Reading, having friends over, and playing on the trampoline
FAVORITE BOOK: *Little House on the Prairie* by Laura I. Wilder
FAVORITE MOVIE: *Beauty and the Beast*
PET PEEVE: "Rick" (a boy at school)

BRENNA HOSTBJOR

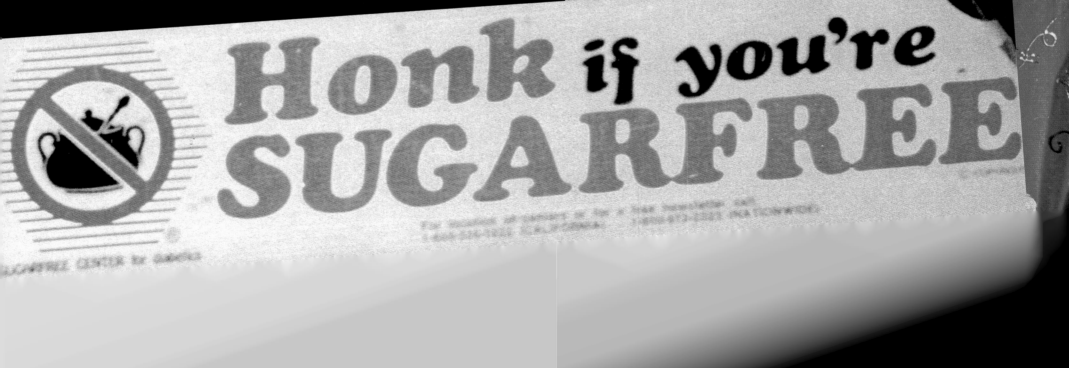

Honk if you're SUGARFREE

AGE: Approximately 45
EDUCATION: (Nine years)
OCCUPATION: Student of many things
FAVORITE PASTIMES: Hiking, learning about ways of life, religion, politics, ideas, and music
FAVORITE BOOK: *Les Misérables* by Victor Hugo
FAVORITE MOVIE: Western movies, because of the scenery
PET PEEVE: Untruthfulness and exploitation

ZEUS COSMOS

Author's Note: When I interviewed him, Zeus was parked and "camping" right next to the White House. He says he's been living in his Volvo for 21 years.

VE ARE HELPING STOP ROUTINE CIRCUMCISION

BUMPER STICKER *Wisdom*   "**Don't laugh—rent is too high**": "Well, I tell you, I don't like to live in downtown slums, where there is a lot of crime, and crowded places, but those are the cheapest places you can get to live. To find a reasonable humane place that is healthy for your spirit and your body to live, you have to live out in the suburbs, and rent out there is very expensive. So, if I had a place out in the suburbs, a decent place. But they want a lot of money and it's expensive and I cannot afford all this rent, so I found myself sleeping outside. My car is loaded, as you see, because I've been living outside for a long time. I've spent a lot of time in the national forests and national monuments. I am a nature worshiper. I come to the cities to learn about historical things, educational things, like museums. Washington, D.C., has a lot of museums. A lot of times I go to university towns because lectures are open to the public. I've been living like this since 1973."

"**We are helping stop routine circumcision**": "Circumcision is a very bad thing. It has no medical reasons. It is extremely cruel to do that to the baby, and it maims the baby for life. They lose sensitivity from the organ without the foreskin. It is extremely inhumane to do that. Try to picture a baby tied up to a table with his legs and hands strapped and cutting him off and bleeding him up, and the baby is screaming and the baby is maimed for the rest of his life. On top of that you have these liars who tell you it is medically needed, which is not true. Don't listen to these liars and don't let your baby be cut up. Nature made the body to be perfect. It took nine months and millions of years to develop that foreskin, and you don't need an idiot to cut it off because of his sick belief. You don't have to cut your foreskin off any more than cut your ears off."

CAROL EVERETT

AGE: 37
EDUCATION: Business Computer Training Institute
OCCUPATION: Homemaker
FAVORITE PASTIMES: Disc golf, bowling, and gardening
FAVORITE BOOK: *The Bridges of Madison County* by Robert James Waller
FAVORITE MOVIE: *Gone with the Wind*
PET PEEVE: People who don't listen

BUMPER STICKER *Wisdom* "Well, sometimes I'm a very aggressive driver, and I get so upset with bad drivers—especially when drivers turn right without signaling or when they pull out in front of me and then turn off right at the next driveway. It took me a long time to find something to put on my van, because bumper stickers are a very public thing. I wanted mine to say just how I feel."

STRESS: The confusion created when one's mind over-rides the body's natural desire to choke the living shit out of some asshole who desperately needs it!

PLANET EARTH C

SKU 992877

STRESS: The confusion created when one's mind over-rides the body's natural desire to choke the living shit out of some asshole who desperately needs it!

GRACE AMADOR

I may be fat, but you're ugly, and I can diet.

BUMPER STICKER *Wisdom* "My daughter, Wendy, bought it for me. My weight goes up and down, and she thought it was funny. Wendy's bumper stickers say 'Shop till you drop' and 'I'm a bitch.' She gripes about everything."

I may be fat, but you're ugly, and I can diet.

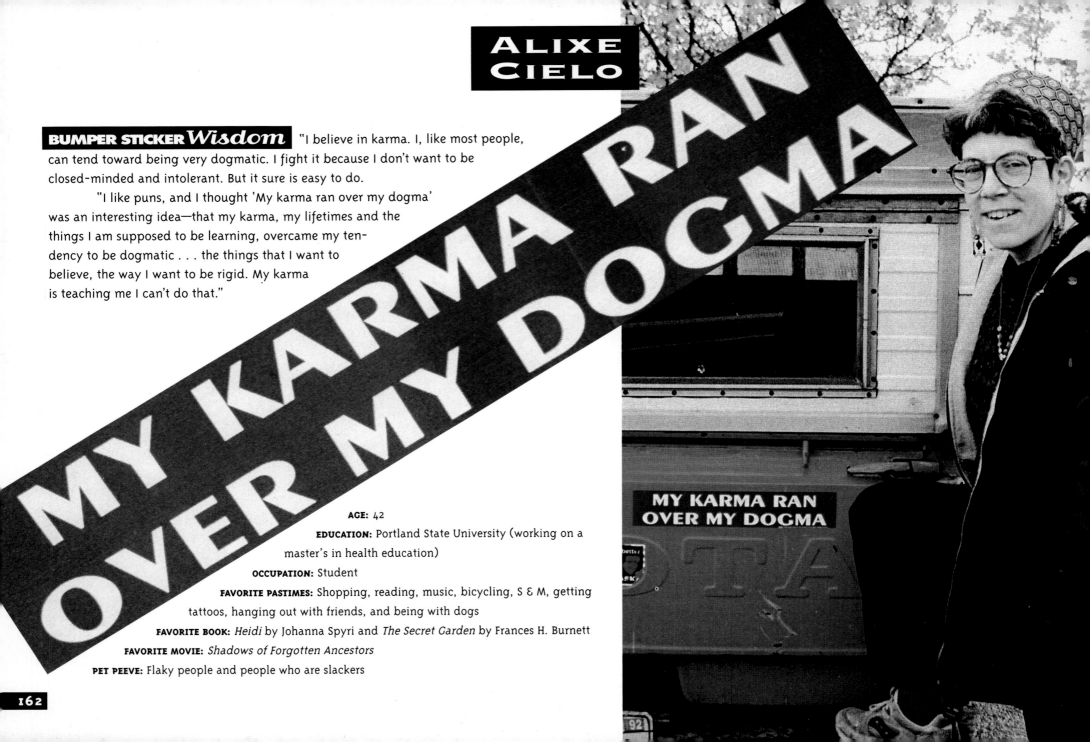

ALIXE CIELO

BUMPER STICKER *Wisdom* "I believe in karma. I, like most people, can tend toward being very dogmatic. I fight it because I don't want to be closed-minded and intolerant. But it sure is easy to do.

"I like puns, and I thought 'My karma ran over my dogma' was an interesting idea—that my karma, my lifetimes and the things I am supposed to be learning, overcame my tendency to be dogmatic . . . the things that I want to believe, the way I want to be rigid. My karma is teaching me I can't do that."

MY KARMA RAN OVER MY DOGMA

AGE: 42

EDUCATION: Portland State University (working on a master's in health education)

OCCUPATION: Student

FAVORITE PASTIMES: Shopping, reading, music, bicycling, S & M, getting tattoos, hanging out with friends, and being with dogs

FAVORITE BOOK: *Heidi* by Johanna Spyri and *The Secret Garden* by Frances H. Burnett

FAVORITE MOVIE: *Shadows of Forgotten Ancestors*

PET PEEVE: Flaky people and people who are slackers

MY KARMA RAN OVER MY DOGMA

ELIZABETH FOX

AGE: 42
EDUCATION: Boston University (Ph.D. in English literature)
OCCUPATION: Teacher at Massachusetts College of Pharmacy and Allied Health Sciences
FAVORITE PASTIMES: Reading, writing, movies, visiting museums, and sports
FAVORITE BOOK: *Psychoanalysis and Feminism* by Juliet Mitchell and *Sons and Lovers* by D. H. Lawrence
PET PEEVE: Selfishness and smugness

BUMPER STICKER *Wisdom* "The bumper sticker is perfect for me because it is theoretical and therefore has wide implications. To 'Subvert the dominant paradigm' is to open one's self to other ways of approaching something. That's the only way we make breakthroughs. For me, it's particularly aimed against patriarchy. I think that is the dominant paradigm—and an especially oppressive one.

"I think there is something playful in the bumper sticker too, because *subvert* is a Latinate way to say, 'Change things around,' 'Flip it over,' 'Juggle.' Juggle what you think. Juggle your way out of looking at things. Make a kaleidoscope of your mind. The paradigm is just a model.

"Last summer I was in Dartmouth and a woman stopped me and said she loved the bumper sticker. She was a witch, sort of a pagan witch, and she thought it was terrific and it made her laugh.

"'Subvert the dominant paradigm' just means there's an element of uncertainty in whatever is dominant. Life is much more complex than we can usually formulate."

SUBVERT THE DOMINANT PARADIGM

PAPA JOHN O'BRIEN
(ALIAS SANTA CLAUS)

AGE: 63
EDUCATION: Polytechnic High School
OCCUPATION: Santa Claus
FAVORITE PASTIMES: Old cars, collecting pop tabs, being married, and grandchildren
FAVORITE BOOK: Trucking magazines
FAVORITE MOVIE: *Planes, Trains & Automobiles*
PET PEEVE: People who can't convey the truth to you face-to-face

BUMPER STICKER *Wisdom*

"I like being Santa Claus, and I figured that it gives people a little laugh, and since I am built the way I am, I figured that it was appropriate at the time."

Author's Note: *Here is a chance to see what Santa looks like without his red suit. I caught him shopping at the Big R. His other bumper sticker reads "If reindeer really can fly . . . our windshields are in big trouble."*

KNOW WHY SANTA WEARS A RED SUIT?
CAUSE FAT PEOPLE DON'T LOOK GOOD NAKED

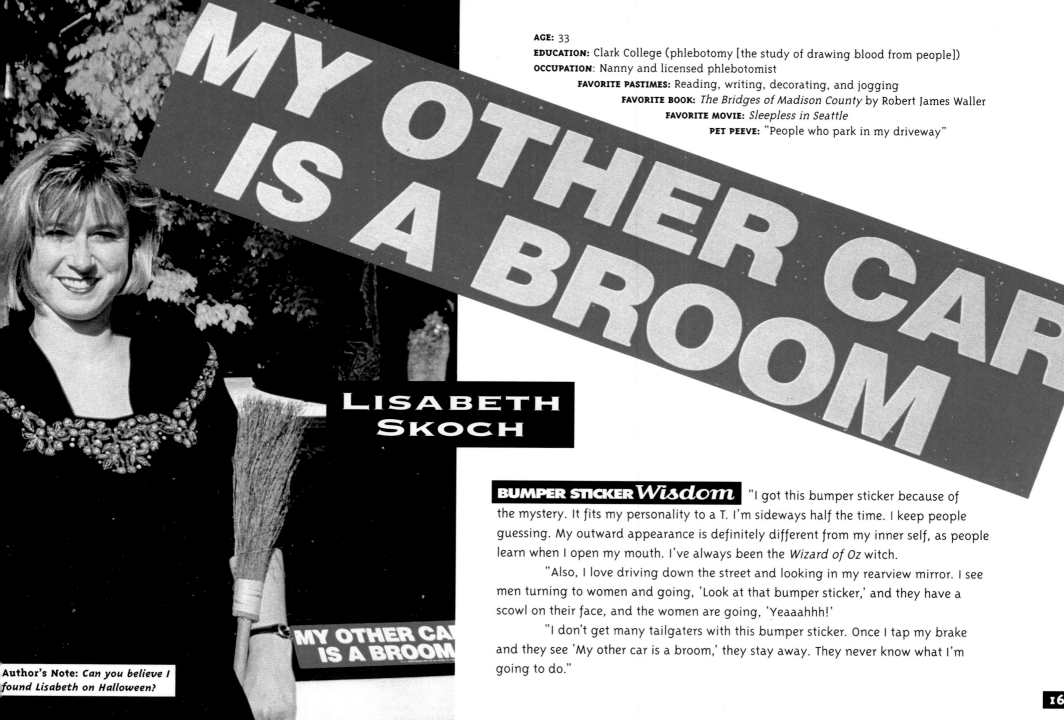

MY OTHER CAR IS A BROOM

LISABETH SKOCH

AGE: 33
EDUCATION: Clark College (phlebotomy [the study of drawing blood from people])
OCCUPATION: Nanny and licensed phlebotomist
FAVORITE PASTIMES: Reading, writing, decorating, and jogging
FAVORITE BOOK: *The Bridges of Madison County* by Robert James Waller
FAVORITE MOVIE: *Sleepless in Seattle*
PET PEEVE: "People who park in my driveway"

BUMPER STICKER *Wisdom* "I got this bumper sticker because of the mystery. It fits my personality to a T. I'm sideways half the time. I keep people guessing. My outward appearance is definitely different from my inner self, as people learn when I open my mouth. I've always been the *Wizard of Oz* witch.

"Also, I love driving down the street and looking in my rearview mirror. I see men turning to women and going, 'Look at that bumper sticker,' and they have a scowl on their face, and the women are going, 'Yeaaahhh!'

"I don't get many tailgaters with this bumper sticker. Once I tap my brake and they see 'My other car is a broom,' they stay away. They never know what I'm going to do."

Author's Note: *Can you believe I found Lisabeth on Halloween?*

MY OTHER CAR IS A BROOM

DEBBIE MÜLLER

AGE: 33
EDUCATION: Chemeketa Community College (nursing)
OCCUPATION: Registered nurse
FAVORITE PASTIMES: Bicycling and "being with my husband, our two-year-old son, and our dog"
FAVORITE BOOK: *Watership Down* by Richard Adams
FAVORITE MOVIE: *The Wizard of Oz*
PET PEEVE: Slow drivers on narrow two-lane roads

BUMPER STICKER *Wisdom* "I got the bumper sticker 'The weather is here, wish you were beautiful' because I thought it was funny. I've since found out that Jimmy Buffett has a song that has that line in it. A lot of people identify with it that way.

"I was just getting a divorce, and it was just sarcastic enough."

THE WEATHER IS HERE, WISH YOU WERE BEAUTIFUL

DIE YUPPIE SCUM

AVENGE YOURSELF -
Live Long Enough To Be A
Problem To Your Children

RUNNING ON
EMPTY
(LIFE, DEATH, AND THE LAST WORD)

GET EVEN —
DIE IN DEBT

EAT WELL, STAY FIT,
DIE ANYWAY
R.I.P.

Don't take life too
seriously, it isn't
PERMANENT

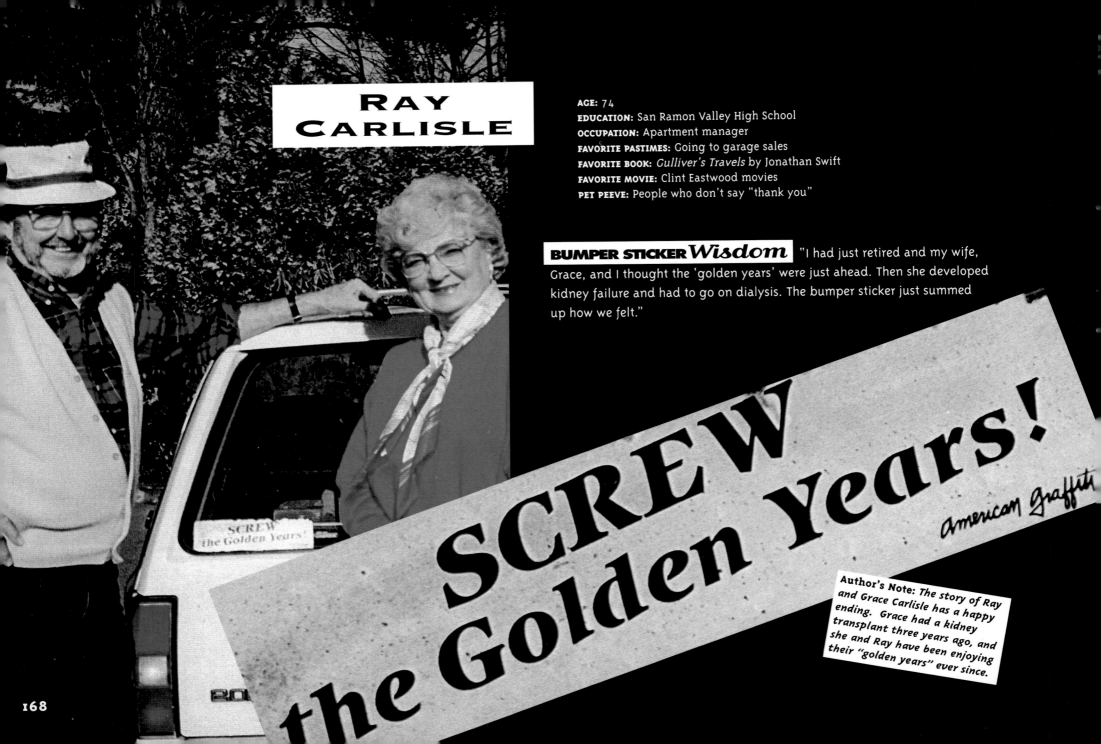

RAY CARLISLE

AGE: 74
EDUCATION: San Ramon Valley High School
OCCUPATION: Apartment manager
FAVORITE PASTIMES: Going to garage sales
FAVORITE BOOK: *Gulliver's Travels* by Jonathan Swift
FAVORITE MOVIE: Clint Eastwood movies
PET PEEVE: People who don't say "thank you"

BUMPER STICKER *Wisdom* "I had just retired and my wife, Grace, and I thought the 'golden years' were just ahead. Then she developed kidney failure and had to go on dialysis. The bumper sticker just summed up how we felt."

SCREW the Golden Years!

American Graffiti

Author's Note: The story of Ray and Grace Carlisle has a happy ending. Grace had a kidney transplant three years ago, and she and Ray have been enjoying their "golden years" ever since.

WILLIAM H. HARRIS

AGE: 67
EDUCATION: Liberal High School
OCCUPATION: Retired head of maintenance for a nursing home
FAVORITE PASTIMES: Fishing for catfish
FAVORITE BOOK: Westerns by Zane Grey
FAVORITE MOVIE: *Long Journey Home*
PET PEEVE: "None, really."

BUMPER STICKER *Wisdom* "Well, when I seen it I knew I had to have it because that has been my luck for most of my life. Just when I thought I was going to get ahead, why, something always happened. So I bought it and it's been on my pickup about ten years. When my wife and I moved out here to western Kansas, and she was working at the nursing home, and I was too, and we bought a new pickup, new camper, and bought us a new home, and we thought we were really getting ready to go somewhere, and she took sick. We discovered she had terminal cancer. She only lived about eight months. That one there, it really threw me for a loop. Just when I thought I was going to get ahead, why, then I got set back. But I'm thankful for what I do have. I'm retired now, able to pay my bills, and—I don't have any money, but, shoot, if you had it, what could you do?"

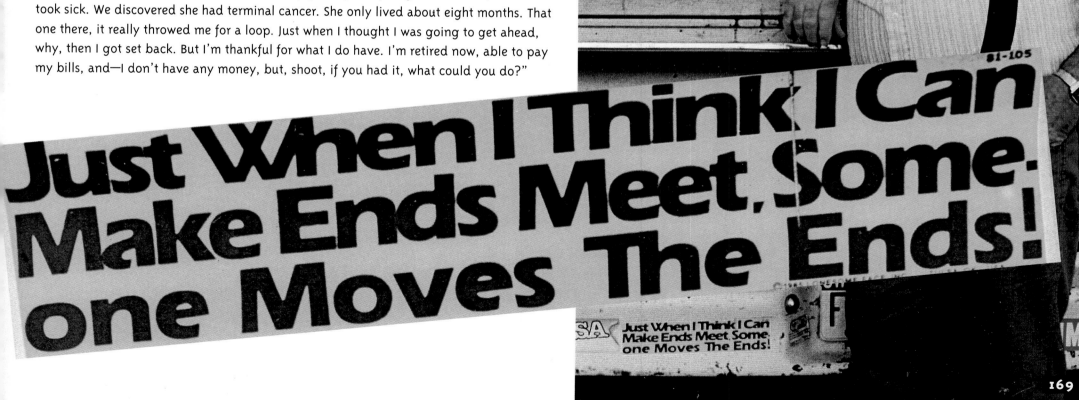

Just When I Think I Can Make Ends Meet, Someone Moves The Ends!

LIFE IS HARD THEN YOU DIE

LIFE IS HARD
THEN YOU DIE.

AGE: 51
EDUCATION: Clackamas Community College (police science)
OCCUPATION: Retired state patrolman
FAVORITE PASTIMES: Fishing and wood carving
FAVORITE BOOK: Nonfiction war novels about Vietnam and the Korean War
FAVORITE MOVIE: *A Few Good Men*
PET PEEVE: Drunk drivers

JIM HASTINGS

BUMPER STICKER *Wisdom* "I bought this bumper sticker 12 years ago in Utah. I don't know what they made it out of, but it sure has lasted. The bumper sticker says it all. There should be a second half to that: 'Life is hard . . . then you die . . . and nobody said it was going to be easy.'"

TRISHA A. DUNN

AGE: 44
EDUCATION: Eastern Washington State College (education)
OCCUPATION: Single parent, pursuing a career in marketing, and a waitress
FAVORITE PASTIMES: Dancing, reading, sewing, gardening, creating, and arts and crafts
FAVORITE BOOK: *You Can't Afford the Luxury of Negative Thought* by John-Roger and Peter McWilliams
FAVORITE MOVIE: Bob Hope, Bing Crosby, and Fred Astaire movies
PET PEEVE: Critical intolerance

BUMPER STICKER *Wisdom* "Basically, what 'Enjoy life—this is not a rehearsal!' tells me is that life really is a wonderful experience. It's something to be treasured and enjoyed. Don't take it so hard. Enjoy the moment. It's a spiritual concept for me. It's a matter of embracing myself with a sense of wonderment, and just trying to be thoughtful and loving and caring.

"For example, when I'm driving on the freeway and it's really crowded, instead of getting angry with the guy in front of me, I look around and see that, gosh, it's beautiful, the trees are blooming—things like that.

"Try to get away from the negative. Respect yourself and enjoy life."

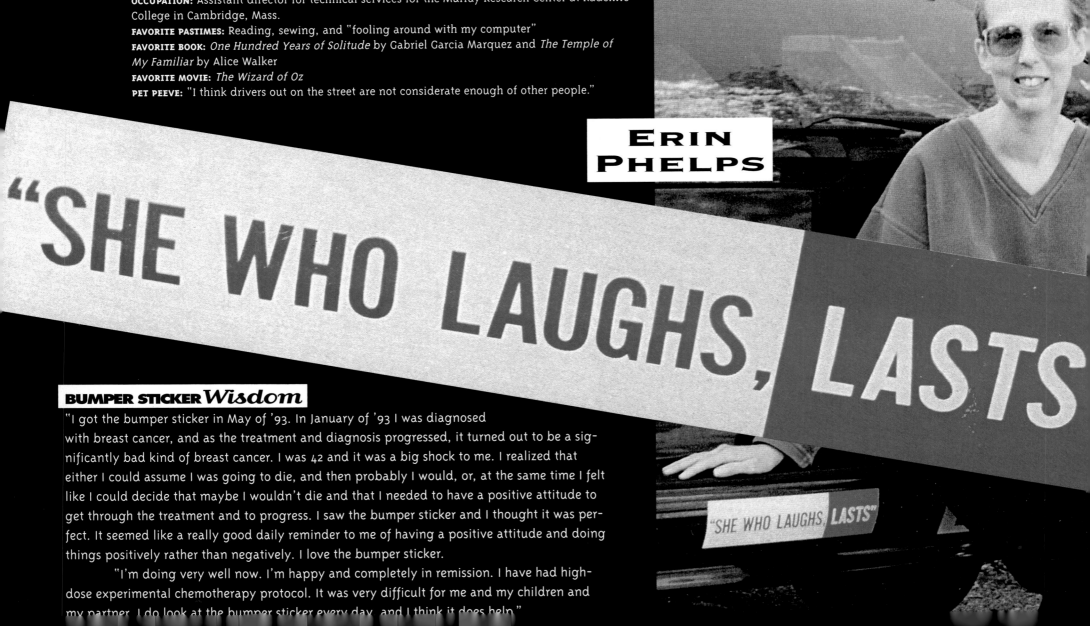

AGE: 43

EDUCATION: Harvard School of Education (Ph.D.)

OCCUPATION: Assistant director for technical services for the Murray Research Center at Radcliffe College in Cambridge, Mass.

FAVORITE PASTIMES: Reading, sewing, and "fooling around with my computer"

FAVORITE BOOK: *One Hundred Years of Solitude* by Gabriel Garcia Marquez and *The Temple of My Familiar* by Alice Walker

FAVORITE MOVIE: *The Wizard of Oz*

PET PEEVE: "I think drivers out on the street are not considerate enough of other people."

ERIN PHELPS

"SHE WHO LAUGHS, LASTS"

BUMPER STICKER *Wisdom*

"I got the bumper sticker in May of '93. In January of '93 I was diagnosed with breast cancer, and as the treatment and diagnosis progressed, it turned out to be a significantly bad kind of breast cancer. I was 42 and it was a big shock to me. I realized that either I could assume I was going to die, and then probably I would, or, at the same time I felt like I could decide that maybe I wouldn't die and that I needed to have a positive attitude to get through the treatment and to progress. I saw the bumper sticker and I thought it was perfect. It seemed like a really good daily reminder to me of having a positive attitude and doing things positively rather than negatively. I love the bumper sticker.

"I'm doing very well now. I'm happy and completely in remission. I have had high-dose experimental chemotherapy protocol. It was very difficult for me and my children and my partner. I do look at the bumper sticker every day, and I think it does help."

BUMPER STICKER Wisdom

America's Pulpit Above the Tailpipe

AGE: 48
EDUCATION: University of Oregon (foreign languages and journalism)
OCCUPATION: Graphic designer
FAVORITE PASTIMES: Photography, enjoying the out-of-doors, horseback riding, spending time with family, and reading and writing about American culture
FAVORITE BOOK: *Angle of Repose* by Wallace Stegner
FAVORITE MOVIE: *A River Runs Through It*
PET PEEVE: Windsniffers

BUMPER STICKER *Wisdom* "I hope *Bumper Sticker Wisdom* has been helpful and fun for the reader, for it has been wondrously enjoyable to write. I started with a desire to better understand bumper stickers and the people and perspectives behind them. In particular I searched out bumper stickers that made me think, laugh, or wonder.

"In the process I came to learn more of myself. First, that I had been moving in a circle of friends that, from comparative perspective, seemed like-minded and homogeneous. Second, that contemporary America is indeed peopled by a remarkably diverse array of individuals, often with conflicting and strongly held views. Finally—and most importantly—people may hold diametrically opposing views and still be good people. I found I really liked individuals with whom I strongly disagreed on one or another issue. So my conclusion is this: It's great to speak out. It's OK to disagree. It's healthy to respect and leave room for other perspectives and for humanity and humor. Maybe tolerance is the ultimate bumper sticker wisdom."

CAROL GARDNER

BUMPER STICKER *Wisdom*

The following bumper stickers may be ordered by contacting the merchants listed next to them:

Fight crime—shoot back

Citizens Committee for the Right to Keep and Bear Arms
12500 NE Tenth Place
Bellevue, WA 98005
(206) 454-4911 or fax: (206) 451-3959

Wild women don't get the blues
God is coming and is she pissed
Against abortion? Don't have one!
A woman without a man is like a fish without a bicycle
Rush is Reich
Visualize world peace

Northern Sun Merchandising
2916 E Lake
Minneapolis, MN 55406
(612) 729-2001

God bless the IRS, without them I'd be filthy rich!

One Liners
P.O. Box 781
Simi Valley, CA 93062

Jesus loves you, but everyone else thinks you're an asshole
Fahrfenäked
The first boat people were white
Vacuuming sucks
I'd rather be fishing, and I don't even like it
Sex is like pizza! Even when it's bad it's kinda good

Phresh Stickers
43 NW 1st Avenue
Portland, OR 97209
(503) 285-6539
For a catalog, send name, address, and $1 or SASE

Share the heritage—take a kid hunting

Texas Wildlife Association
1635 NE Loop 410, #108
San Antonio, TX 78209
(210) 826-2904

Other Books from Beyond Words Publishing, Inc.

REEL WOMEN: The World of Women Who Fish

by Lyla Foggia, $24.95, hardcover

For the more than 18.6 million American women who fish, *Reel Women* is the first-ever comprehensive history of women and angling, from fly fishing to big-game saltwater. It offers an illuminating journey into this formerly invisible dynasty of remarkable women and their astounding achievements, from 1496 to present, with rare photographs and an indispensable resource directory enabling women to network locally and nationally. Dame Juliana Berners is reported to have written the first treatise on fishing in the English language, published in 1496. Now, 500 years later, author Lyla Foggia (herself an avid angler) presents compelling biographies of women anglers and a state-by-state directory of fishing resources designed by or for women.

LETTERS FROM THE LIGHT: An Afterlife Journal from the Self-Lighted World

written through the hand of Elsa Barker; edited by Kathy Hart, $18.95, hardcover

A man dies; a woman thousands of miles away begins a process of "automatic writing." The message he sends through her is a description of life after death: a reassurance that there is nothing to fear in death and that the life after this one is similar in many ways to the one we already know. Readers invariably concur that the book eliminates their fear of dying. *Letters from the Light* was originally written and published more than eighty years ago.

HINDSIGHTS: The Wisdom and Breakthroughs of Remarkable People

by Guy Kawasaki, $22.95, hardcover

What have you learned from your life that you would like to share with the next generation? Get a fresh appreciation of the human experience in this inspirational collection of interviews with thirty-three people who have overcome unique challenges. They are candid about their failures and disappointments, and insightful about turning adversity into opportunity. Guy Kawasaki spent over two years researching and interviewing such people as Apple Computer co-founder Steve Wozniak, management guru Tom Peters, and entrepreneur Mary Kay. But not everyone in the book is a celebrity. They share their revelations and life experiences, motivating the reader for both personal and professional growth.

THERE'S A HOLE IN MY SIDEWALK: The Romance of Self-Discovery

by Portia Nelson, $7.95, softcover

A timeless self-help book of prose-poetry. In this candid and delightful journey through emotional and psychological healing, Ms. Nelson guides the reader through the stages of a sometimes terrifying, always fascinating, and undeniably authentic courtship with the self. A valuable tool for opening dialogue internally and with others, this book is used worldwide by 12-step groups and therapists who find it helpful on the path of individual healing. You will find yourself rereading this book many times. Includes the well-loved "Autobiography in Five Short Chapters." A poster of this verse is also available.

To order or to request a catalog, contact

Beyond Words Publishing, Inc.

4443 NE Airport Road, Hillsboro, OR 97124-6074

503-693-8700 or 1-800-284-9673

If you have seen a bumper sticker that caught your eye but that didn't make this book,
or
If you have an idea for a bumper sticker that you've never seen before,
or
If you have a bumper sticker that you think should have been in this book,

You may be included in *Bumper Sticker Wisdom II.*

Please contact Carol W. Gardner at 1-800-817-6864.